"*Stairway Walks in San Francisco* is a wonderfully informative guidebook, custom-made for a city with challenging hills and picture-perfect views. Painstakingly indexed and chock full of fascinating details...an exciting and valuable resource for lifelong residents and first-time visitors alike."

—*Travel Books Review*

"Adah Bakalinsky...[one of] a breed of highly knowledgeable, professional tour masters who can yank back the dull scrim of ordinary perceptions and enrich our understanding of what goes on all around us."

—*CSAA Motorland Magazine*

"During each walk, [Adah] explores a whole neighborhood, making stairways a focal point. Her knowledge of individual areas—their history, geology, and denizens—is encyclopedic."

—*Image Magazine*

"Bakalinsky has been scouring the city since the mid-1970s, clambering, walking, exploring tiny alleys and stairways, grand steps, paths and risers that interlace the city. She has carried her love of the stairways into...*Stairway Walks of San Francisco*."

—*San Diego Union-Tribune*

"Bakalinsky knows the streets of San Francisco—and the hundreds of stairways connecting them—better than anyone alive. Stairway Walks...remains one of the most entertaining and informative of all San Francisco tour books."

—*The Review*

"There are more than 350...flights of steps traversing the city's hills, and no one knows them more intimately than Adah Bakalinsky, San Francisco's unofficial chairwoman of stairs."

—*Walking Magazine*

In memory of
Trudy Douglas (1907–1995)
who created the original pen and ink drawings
and
Gene Smith (1916–1999)
who created working maps and editorial order

Pemberton Street

Stairway Walks in San Francisco

Adah Bakalinsky

WILDERNESS PRESS
BERKELEY

THIRD EDITION April 1995
Second printing November 1995
Third printing October 1998
FOURTH EDITION September 2001

Drawings by Trudie Douglas (*pp. 12, 22, 39, 47, 58, 71, 94, 111, 123, 131, 156, 164*) and Modesto Ortega (*pp. iv, 78, 100*)
Maps by Pat Beebee, Ben Pease, and Terry Milne
Front cover photo by Arden Danekas
            (*photo manipulated by Larry B. Van Dyke*)
Author photo (*back cover*) by Ralph Colby
Book and cover design by Larry B. Van Dyke

Library of Congress Card Catalog Number 2001045320
International Standard Book Number 0-89997-275-6

Manufactured in the United States of America

Published by **Wilderness Press**
            1200 5th Street
            Berkeley, CA 94710
            (800) 443-7227
            FAX (510) 558-1696
            mail@wildernesspress.com
            www.wildernesspress.com
Contact us for a free catalog

♻ Printed on recycled paper, 20% post-consumer waste

Library of Congress Cataloging-in-Publication Data

Bakalinsky, Adah.
    Stairway walks in San Francisco / Adah Bakalinsky.--4th ed.
        p. cm.
    Includes bibliographical references and index.
    ISBN 0-89997-275-6
        1. San Francisco (Calif.)--Tours. 2. Walking--California--San Francisco--Guidebooks.
    3. Stairs--California--San Francisco--Guidebooks. I. Title.
    F869.S33 B35 2001
    917.94'610454--dc21

                                                2001045320

Dedications

This book, in all editions, is dedicated to Max, who can make a walk to the grocery store an adventure; to our parents, Morris and Helen Packerman, and Joseph and Selma Bakalinsky; to our children, Eric, Polly, Mimi, and Alan; and to our grandchildren, Noah, Kieran, and Alyssa—all good walkers.

The 4th edition of *Stairway Walks in San Francisco* is dedicated to John Olmsted, who introduced me to the extraordinary, mythic, nature-designed, wonder of wonders of *stairways*—the Jug Handle Giant Ecological Staircase in Mendocino County. The five staircase terraces along Jug Handle Creek are recognized as the best-preserved ecological showcase of coastal evolution in North America. Each of the terraces of the Staircase was carved into the greywacke sandstone by ocean waves, and each is roughly 100,000 years older than the one below it.

Today, the terraces display distinctly different plant communities in an ordered sequence: from natural grasslands to giant forests of pine, fir, spruce, and finally the dwarfed cypresses and Bolander pines that make up the famous Pygmy Forest. John is the founder of the California Institute of Man in Nature (CIMIN). The purpose of the Institute is to restore and preserve a living thread of the original landscapes across California, as John Muir had dreamed it, before it is totally demolished.

John believes the wilderness should be accessible, where possible, to disabled visitors. Toward that objective, he founded the offshoot Sequoya Challenge group that helped complete South Yuba Independence Trail and Jug Handle Independence Trail. My heartfelt thanks to you, John. I consider you today's John Muir. For information about visiting and exploring Jug Handle State Reserve call (707) 937-5804 or (707) 964-4630. For information about South Yuba Independence Trail call (916) 272-3823.

Arden Danekas

Contents

Acknowledgments

I was fortunate while growing up to live near my grandparents in a neighborhood where everybody walked. I remember walking with them to the synagogue, the butcher, the baker, and to visit family friends. My aunts walked to work, and my treat was to accompany them to a halfway point. Everybody in my family walked. When I began piano lessons and had to use the streetcars, I experienced motion sickness.

San Francisco is the perfect place for me. I enjoy the weather. I never tire of exploring the neighborhoods and walking the hills. I always find someone to talk with who shares another portion of San Francisco history with me.

Among those who have told me neighborhood stories and given me a sense of the place are F. Joseph Butler, Sam Chicos, Ina Cokeley, Evelyn Crawford, David Graves, Esther Grover, Raymond Isola, Donna Leimbach, Harold Levy, Pari Livermore, and Anna Prusow.

I have found generosity among friends who took the time to accompany me to special sections of their neighborhoods. Among them are Bob Buckles, Felix Ecker, Simone Edwards, Esther Feinberg, Ruth McGlashan, Dawn Murayama, Louise Meyer, Ruth Passen, Amy Powell, Evelyn Schaugaard, Al Selinger, and Tom Serchen.

Throughout the years I have found many kindred walkers who love urban exploring. They share their discoveries, they critique my walks, and they accompany me, or scout for me. I need to know how various types of walkers walk a route before I make the final design and the decision to include it in the book.

I thank Ruth Allen, Monique and Jeff Baker, Buzz Brooks, Germano Corazza, Adele and Bob Donn, Gene Edwards, Peter Feltzer, Nikki Goldsborough, Renate and Ron Kay, Kim Mayor, Jack Milburn, Mildred Oliva, John and Gertrud Remak, Lottie Ross, Judith Serin, Marilyn Straka, and Dale Tillery.

For specialized information, I am grateful to Mel Baker, Barbara Bunschu, Tom Potts, Ron Rod, Carol Talpers, Virginia Tanzer, and Tom

Tazelaar. It was very rewarding to talk with people from various groups and City departments who are working to improve and maintain the liveability of San Francisco: Chris Buck, Friends of the Urban Forest; Christopher Campbell, Natural Areas Management, Dept. of Recreation and Parks; Tom Carey and Susan Goldstein, San Francisco Room of the Public Library; Margaret Goodale, Randall Jr. Museum; Bob Holloway, GGNRA Interpretive Park Ranger; Nan McGuire, SLUG; Wolfgang Schubert and Rich Harnett, GGNRA Docents; Stephen Shotland, San Francisco Planning Dept.; and Isabel Wade, Neighborhood Parks Council.

I want to recognize Terry Milne, Bernal Heights resident and activist, who designed the two Bernal Heights walks to include new stairways, updated several maps and the list of City-wide stairways; and Dennis Downing who worked, with his Upper Noe Valley neighbors and the Department of Public Works, for five years to acquire the new upper section of the 27th St. Stairway. I am indebited to Michael Lampen, historian and geologist, and Ben Pease, trail blazer and cartographer, for their generosity of spirit in sharing their knowledge and research, and allowing me to modify what I needed for Walk 1 and Walk 20.

The short digressions that appear in the following walks have been selected from my vast collection of "walking" quotes, which I've compiled over the years. Though I can no longer pinpoint many of the sources, they are all either from verifiable magazines and histories, or from authors I've read. I collected them with the idea of having an imaginary dinner party, with each guest being one of these characters.

—Adah Bakalinsky
San Francisco

A Note on Safe Stairway Walking

The fact that a route is described in this book is not a representation that it will be safe at all times and for all persons. Routes vary greatly in difficulty and in the degree of conditioning and agility one needs to enjoy them safely. On some stairway walks, routes may have changed or conditions may have deteriorated since the descriptions were written. Conditions can change owing to weather and other factors—from new construction to earthquakes and mud slides. A stairway trail that is safe on a dry day may prove to be more of a challenge on a rainy day. Use good judgment and minimize your risks on any stairway walk or urban hike by being knowledgeable, prepared, and alert.

Forward & Onward

FOREWORD BY WILLY WERBY

& Upward

When Adah first told me she was doing a book on the stairway walks of San Francisco, my response was some variation of the clueless, "You're kidding!" Well, she wasn't, and her unique concept eventually met with four editions-worth of enthusiasm—even from me.

Because, whether you live in San Francisco or are only passing through, walking our stairways is a wonderfully unusual way of viewing the City.

The best thing is to tag along with Adah, for whom each walk is an adventure. Neighborhood stories, details of flora and architecture, transient items that float across our line of vision, catch her attention. Along the route, hidden from sight of the street, are any number of delightful surprises. And San Franciscans, a friendly lot, sometimes invite us inside their hillside houses to share their pleasure of a view or a thriving garden.

The next best thing is to arm yourself with this book and make your own discoveries. And no Stairmaster has such spectacular views.

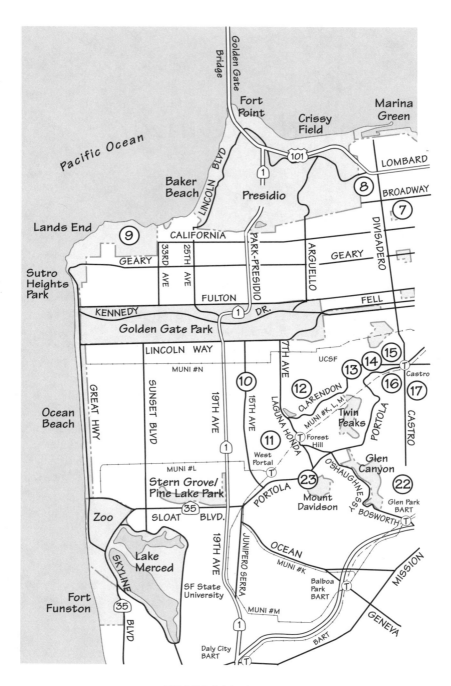

WALK LOCATOR MAP

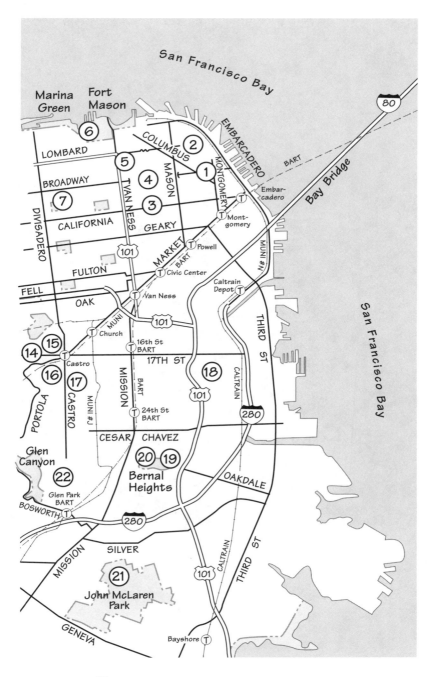

(10) Circled numbers refer to walk locations

Potrero Hill—circa 1950

Introduction

The natural habitat of a stairway is a hill. Those of us who love stairways cherish the image of the unknown walker of eons ago, who, walking in the indentations in the sides of the cliff, visualized them as a welcome shortcut up the hill. Exercising ingenuity and mathematical skill, this walker developed the principle of comfortable stairways.

San Francisco is a "walking city." Built upon forty-two hills, it is surrounded by the Bay on the east, the Pacific on the west, a peninsula on the south, and on the north, the Golden Gate. Within those confines, variety is constant. Light and water combine to produce striking effects on bridges and buildings throughout the day; at sunset, the beams of light highlight the hills and sides of houses.

The hills accelerate changes in perspective as one walks around corners or circles the ridges. Landmarks recede and suddenly emerge in a landscape abounding in inclines and angled streets. The Mt. Sutro TV tower viewed from the mid-Sunset District is a beautiful sky sculpture; from the Sutro area, it looks like a ship in space. From Ashbury Heights, it looks pedestrian. It appears large and within touching distance from the outer Sunset District; walk two blocks toward it, and it appears distant and small.

The streets of San Francisco range from comparatively flat, such as Irving, to almost vertical, such as sections of Duboce and Filbert and Duncan. In fact, the City Fathers and developers found grading the streets a primary obstacle in converting San Francisco from a tent town into a city of timbered houses. Some of the hills were completely demolished in the process; others were cut into without much planning. When the task seemed insurmountable, the "street" ended.

How does one maneuver from one street level to another when there are so many hills? Via stairways, of course! There are more than 400 stairways of all descriptions: crooked, straight, short, long, concrete, wood, balustraded, and unadorned. Paved streets often follow the contours of hills, but the stairways allow direct vertical access from one street to another. They are one of the least celebrated aspects of San Francisco. Some of the stairways are not easily identified. One must look on the sidewalk to see if the name is embedded in the concrete.

The 23 walks in the book vary in length and elevation. They are designed for the curious walker. Each walk takes two to two and one-half hours if you enjoy all the sights, scents, and sounds along the way. While Pacific Heights, Russian Hill, and other well-known areas are included, I have focused more attention on neighborhoods that are not usually featured in guidebooks and not well-known to residents of other San Francisco neighborhoods.

The beginning point of each walk can be reached by public transportation (call 673-MUNI for current information). Buses are available at several points of most walks and alternate routes are occasionally suggested for specific reasons. Some of the walks are quite strenuous, but the rewards of stupendous views and delightful discoveries justify the effort.

I suggest walkers carry the following gear to make the adventure more comfortable: binoculars, a city map, a compass, water, fruit, and layered clothing. I use the directions, left and right, but also the compass points, north, east, south, and west, to provide additional assurance. *Note:* the latest AAA map of San Francisco shows stairways! Not all of them, but some well-known ones around Telegraph Hill and Russian Hill, and a few lesser-known ones.

Several impressions become more distinct as I explore the City. San Francisco is experiencing, in some areas, the last third of the urban cycle of decay, destruction, and regeneration every city goes through (a cycle that usually takes 25 to 30 years). Simultaneously, other areas are in stages 1 and 2. When I began exploring neighborhoods in 1975, there were many empty lots in the Bernal Heights, Forest Knolls, and Glen Park neighborhoods. Now dwellings occupy these sites. There were parking spaces in North Beach and Russian Hill and Telegraph Hill neighborhoods. Now there are none.

The area south of Market around 3rd St. between Mission and Howard is now vibrant with clusters of art galleries surrounding the stunning San Francisco Museum of Modern Art. Yerba Buena Center (the area was a gaping hole for 30 years) is one of the City's showpieces. It includes a museum, a performance hall, and several restaurants, gardens, and sculptures. (In the early days of San Francisco, the same geographic area was also the locale of opera houses and restaurants.)

The Embarcadero has become a delightful place to stroll. It has attractive historic plaques embedded in the concrete sidewalks, and informational kiosks along the way. Canary Island palms have been planted in the center islands. The central Embarcadero has a new surface roadway from Fisherman's Wharf to Pacific Bell Park. New connecting public transportation lines on the Embarcadero provide greater convenience and efficiency for the public. Pier 7 has been renovated and one can walk out 800 feet into the Bay to fish or to sit and watch boats and people and cloud formations, and gray whales (during the past winter they were sighted from here). The Ferry Building will be undergoing long overdue, interior renovation, which should be completed in 2002.

The Mission and Potrero Hill are going through reluctant, traumatic conversions to dot-com industries. Bernal Heights has four new stairways complete with lights, railings, and safety steps. Several more are scheduled for 2001. The Asian Museum (the former Main Library) will be the new Civic Center addition. Some new low-rise, low-cost housing may become available in the neighboring Western Addition.

San Francisco still has some open, unmanicured areas to explore. There has been an increase in the number of parks and playgrounds that have been redesigned and made attractive and user-friendly through additional renovation funds. McLaren Park has new restrooms, inviting areas for picnics, and an unusually handsome amphitheater where one can comfortably sit and watch performances. It is wheelchair accessible. Open Space funding has allowed for the purchase of several hilltop areas in the City.

San Francisco has thousands of views, from panoramic to miniature. Some of the most notable ones are in neighborhoods south of Market. Kite Hill, Corona Hill, Bernal Heights Hill, Potrero Hill, and Beacon St. are outstanding panoramic viewing sites. The miniature views *between* houses are fun to note because of slight changes of perspective as you walk by.

Our street system appears irrational and undisciplined. For instance: there are stairways with no visible name (Diamond Heights area has some). Thomas Bros. maps may list a name that is so obscure, no one has ever heard of it. Some streets halve themselves (Castro), and then appear several blocks later; some streets angle into another (Franconia and Rutledge), others continue to be listed on maps even though they may be blocked off or terminated (Pemberton). However, the city parts fit together. Key streets connect one neighborhood to another, and the hills form a scaffold for the disparate jutting, circular, and rectangular areas.

I want to applaud San Francisco Beautiful, the organization dedicated to creating and maintaining the beauty and viability of the City, for its neighborhood outreach, and its vigilance in promoting policies relating to large public issues of the City.

I also want to applaud SLUG (San Francisco League of Urban Gardeners), for their vital work in introducing young people to an appreciation of the science and art of gardening, to an understanding of the interrelationship of nature and people in an urban society, and to the gratification of working consistently toward a goal.

The descriptions in the chapters were up to date at publication time. However, neighborhoods continually evolve. If you find discrepancies, please notify me at Wilderness Press, and we will incorporate the changes in the next edition.

Treasures

& Digressions

The early Spanish explorers of the 18th Century designated three important foci in the City: religious—Mission Dolores; military—The Presidio; and commercial—Yerba Buena Cove. In this walk we'll explore the commercial area.

You will see buildings that were erected on the edge of the shoreline along the middle third of Yerba Buena Cove, now the financial and commercial section of San Francisco. You walk toward Portsmouth Square, which was the center of the Pueblo of Yerba Buena and now is the center of Chinatown; you continue to the slopes of Telegraph Hill where the 19th Century waterfront workers lived.

The Gold Rush to California was the Outward Bound of the 1800s, the 19th Century rite of passage. It took all of one's ingenuity, statesmanship, business acumen, and physical stamina to survive. San Francisco, the entry point for people coming overland by wagon and around the Horn by ship, had a population of approximately 450 at the first census count in 1847 and approximately 20,000 by the end of 1849.

Gradually, as more families arrived in the City, social services were organized; schools, libraries, and churches were opened; lectures, operas, concerts, readings, and theater were offered.

Telegraph Hill, at 284 feet elevation, extended east to Battery St., near the edge of the Bay, making it difficult to unload cargo. After the east slope of the Hill was quarried, it extended just to the west side of Sansome Street Dock workers living in the small cottages along the hillside used a stairway to go to and from work. During the late 19th Century and early 20th, artists, writers, and actors lived on the hill.

Junius Booth of the famous theater family lived at No. 5 Calhoun. The writer, Charles Warren Stoddard, spent part of his childhood here at No. 287 Union. The hill became a special province due in part to its isolated site.

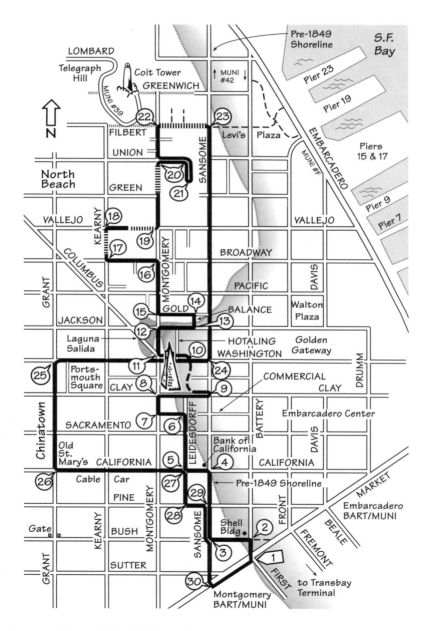

▶ Begin at Market and First (the first street west of Yerba Buena Cove, now about one-half mile from the Ferry Bldg. and the Bay). An interpretive plaque is imbedded in the sidewalk. The Tishman building (1973) at No. 525 Market St. straddles the shoreline.

▶ Cross Market to the intersections of Battery, Bush, and Market. At the corner near the Mechanics Monument is another embedded plaque showing the map of Yerba Buena Cove. The Mechanics Monument was commissioned in 1894 by Peter Donahue to honor

WALK 1: Yerba Buena Cove, Telegraph Hill, & Chinatown Route

Public Transportation: any streetcar, bus, or Metro that runs along Market.

1. Begin at First and Market. Cross Market to the intersection of Battery and Bush.
2. Left on Bush.
3. Right on Sansome to California. Cross to far side.
4. Left on California to Leidesdorff.
5. Right on Leidesdorff to Commercial.
6. Left on Commercial to Montgomery.
7. Right on Montgomery to Clay.
8. Right on Clay, a few yards past Redwood Park to #2 Transamerica Center to see the Niantic plaque.
9. Return to walk through the Park to Washington.
10. Left on Washington to Montgomery.
11. Right on Montgomery to Jackson.
12. Right on Jackson to Balance.
13. Left on Balance to Gold.
14. Left on Gold to Montgomery.
15. Right (north) on Montgomery to Broadway.
16. Left on Broadway to Kearny.
17. Right to ascend Kearny Stwy. to Vallejo.
18. Right to descend Vallejo Stwy. to Montgomery.
19. Left to ascend Montgomery Stwy. to Union.
20. Right turn into Union cul-de-sac. Right turn into Calhoun.
21. Return to Montgomery and turn right to Filbert.
22. Right on Filbert to descend Stwy. to Sansome.
23. Right turn on Sansome to Washington.
24. Right on Washington to right side of Grant to see No. 823 (some hanging purses belonging to the adjoining boutique may hide the number, but it's there).
25. Left (south) on Grant to California.
26. Left on California to Leidesdorff.
27. Right on Leidesdorff to Pine.
28. Left on Pine to Sansome.
29. Right on Sansome to Market.
30. Left on Market to First and your beginning.

his father, James Donahue, founder of Union Iron Works. The foundry, one of the most successful firms in early San Francisco, was located on Harrison St., which provided easy access to the Bay. Douglas Tilden, known as the Michelangelo of the west, sculpted the figures on the monument. Although he had been deaf since childhood, his talent was recognized early, and he was able to study in Paris.

▲ Cross Battery at Bush to see another building that straddles the cove—the 29-story Shell Bldg. at 100 Bush. George Pelham designed and built it in 1929–30. Consistent restoration work has preserved the Art Deco detailing. The shell motif is repeated in the transom, as a light fixture, and in the lobby. At night, the building is suffused with a golden light. You walk over to 130 Bush to see the Heineman Bldg., an anomaly and a curiosity. It is the narrowest building in San Francisco. Three steps into the lobby, and one is almost in the elevator.

▲ Continue west to Sansome, and then north to California. The Bank of California (founded in 1864 by William Ralston and O.J. Mills) straddles the shoreline at No. 400 California. Bliss and Faville designed the existing Beaux Arts style structure in 1907–08. (They also designed the Convent of the Sacred Heart and the St. Francis Hotel.) In 1967 a 21-story tower designed by Anshen and Allen was incorporated into the structure. The integration of the old and new edifices is considered one of the most successful and esthetic in the City. The coffered ceiling is elegant.

▲ Continue west (to your left) on California to the intersection of Leidesdorff, which marks the old shoreline. It was named for Captain William Alexander Leidesdorff, a prosperous businessman, linguist, and Master of the ship, *Julia Ann*, which carried Hawaiian sugar that was traded for California hides. Leidesdorff also was active in fur trading with the Russians at Fort Ross. He settled in Yerba Buena in 1838 and built the City Hotel at Kearny and Clay, and a warehouse on the beach at California and Leidesdorff. The Captain, born of Danish and African ancestry in the Virgin Islands, died of cholera in 1848 at the age of 36.

▲ Walk to your right through Leidesdorff Alley toward Sacramento. Read the plaque that details the history of What Cheer House Hotel (left side of street) built by R.B. Woodward in 1852. He later added a private library and museum for guests, an unusual facility for hotels to offer. Captain Ulysses S. Grant stayed there in 1854.

(Woodward's Gardens near Mission and 14th was the popular outdoor resort in the City in the 1860s.) Laguna Dulce, a freshwater pond fed by a Nob Hill stream, was situated a half block away at Montgomery and Sacramento. It was also the site of an Indian sweathouse.

▶ Continue on Leidesdorff to Commercial St. Turn left to Montgomery to stand in the place where Captain Montgomery sailed up in the USS Portsmouth, in 1846, to claim the Pueblo of Yerba Buena (established in 1839) for the United States. The Mexican government acceded. It was a quiet takeover.

▶ At the end of the narrow street we see Portsmouth Square, the heart and outdoor living room of Chinatown, formerly the center of the Pueblo of Yerba Buena. (There were many hotels and theaters in this area during the 1850s—the Jenny Lind, the Phoenix, the Adelphi, the Italian Theater, and the Chinese theaters were the better known.)

▶ Continue on Montgomery to Clay. At the southeast corner was the Bank of Italy built in 1904. In the early years, the bank used solicitors to sell accounts. Across the street is the Transamerica Pyramid. The original building on this site was the 1853 Montgomery Block, affectionately known as the Monkey Block. Built by architect Gordon Cummings for Henry Halleck, it was also known as Halleck's Folly because it cost $2 million. Four stories high, it had a fish market, grocery, and the Saloon Bank Exchange Bar, where bankers transacted business. (The Pyramid Saloon has the exact replica of the mahogany bar.) In later years law offices and the largest law library in the area were located in the Block. Sun Yat-sen, founder of the Chinese Nationalist movement, had his office here during his exile, around 1911. In the 1920s and 1930s, artists, writers, and dancers rented studio/living quarters here. Among them were Mezzara—the sculptor, who made the first statue of Lincoln, George Sterling—the poet, and Ann Munstock, who brought modern dance to San Francisco from Germany.

▶ The Monkey Block withstood the 1906 earthquake, but was torn down in 1954 for a parking lot. The Transamerica Pyramid built in 1972 superseded the parking lot. Its precarious site on the shoreline necessitated a 9-foot-thick concrete and steel foundation 52 feet below the sidewalk. The Pyramid has become recognized as a San Francisco icon. I like the diminishing space it occupies as it continues upward. Changing art exhibits are on view in the lobby.

➤ Continue right on Clay and walk past the Redwood Park, established by Transamerica for its employees and the public, to No. 2 Transamerica Center to read the Niantic plaque. The Niantic Bldg. at No. 509 Clay was named for the abandoned ship that provided one side of the structure. The crew left for the gold mines in 1849, and the vessel was converted into a hotel. Artifacts from the ship were found during excavation of the Pyramid site and are on display in the lobby of Washington Towers, across the street, at No. 655 Montgomery. You are welcome to go in.

➤ Return to the Park and walk through. It is a popular place for people to bring their lunch and, during the summer, listen to noon jazz concerts. It is also a sculpture garden and has two of my favorite outdoor pieces. The bronze *Puddle Jumpers* by Glenna Goodacre is a group of six children, whose movements–jumping rope, skipping, and hopping–are caught in mid-air and expressed with great joy and abandon. The *Frog Pond* by Richard Clopton is a group of brass frogs that exhibit the same delight in their pool.

➤ Exit the Park to Washington and turn left to Montgomery. It was here in the New York Store, in 1849, that the first regulation mail shipment, which arrived on the steamer *Oregon*, was sorted and dispersed. On the grillwork around the window above the San Wah Bank, next to No. 735 Montgomery, is the Star of David. The building was used as the first synagogue in San Francisco; the Jewish New Year was celebrated there in September 1849.

➤ Turn right on Montgomery to Jackson. The bridge that crossed Laguna Salida, the brackish inlet of the Yerba Buena Cove was located here. At No. 498, you pass the Lucas Turner & Co. Bank of 1853, with its triangular doorway entrance (saloons used these swing doors). General Sherman, famous for his march through Georgia during the Civil War, was director for several years. A historic plaque is on the wall.

➤ During the Gold Rush, Jackson and Montgomery was the center of Little Chile. Chilenos, expert at using the Chile wheel to crush gold-bearing ore, had come to work in the gold mines. The Sydney Ducks—the Australian convict contingent—lived around the base of Telegraph Hill from Filbert, north, between Montgomery and Kearny. The Hounds—a group of New York toughs—lived around Grant and Pacific. The latter two groups were "hate groups," intent on eradicating people from Central and South America. Finally, after a particularly vengeful foray into Little Chile, the Vigilante group of

1851 (who called themselves the Law and Order Party) was formed under Sam Brannan's leadership to combat the plundering and marauding by the Hounds and Ducks.

▶ You are in the Jackson Square Historic District, which encompasses the area from Washington to Pacific and from Columbus to Sansome. The buildings in the 400 block of Jackson withstood the earthquake and fire of 1906, and the street has many of the earliest structures in San Francisco. Continue to the right on Jackson to Balance, the shortest street in the City. As you pass Hotaling Alley, look up at the Pyramid. The Alley was named for A.P. Hotaling's famed saloon and distillery (No. 429 Jackson). The famous two-line verse that was quoted after the quake posed a question:

> "If as they say God spanked the town for being over frisky
> Why did he burn the churches down and save Hotaling's whiskey?"

▶ Turn left on Balance (named for the sunken ship that lies at Jackson and Front) to Gold, one of the numerous alleys in this part of the City. The old three-story brick buildings are still here. On the left is the side door of Stout Books. Turn left on Gold to Montgomery, and then right (north) toward Broadway.

> *During the winter of 1849–50, 50 inches of rain was reported. Montgomery, unpaved and unplanked, was a treacherous thor-oughfare, especially at night. Wagons sank into the mud, and inebriated pedestrians had to be pulled out. An unforgettable event of that winter was the discovery in the mud along Montgomery of three men's bodies.*

▶ The William Stout Architectural bookstore at No. 804 Montgomery has one of the most complete selections in the country of books on architecture, and books relating to architecture. I love to browse here. Japanesque Gallery at No. 824 Montgomery is my favorite stop for an esthetic experience.

▶ Pacific interests me because it illustrates so many contrasts in a few blocks. To our left where No. 549 Pacific stands (at Kearny), the scapula of a mammoth was dug up. Hundreds of thousands of years ago mammoths and bison roamed around here in a wet area that resembled southern Marin County. To our right, the street is lined on both sides, predominately with ficus trees. Behind the trees, the old, 19th Century, three-story brick structures contrast greatly in size to

Filbert Street

the enormous Pyramid and the Bank of California. The old structures have an ambiance of a small town where you could call out the first names of all inhabitants. At the same, time during the Gold Rush days, the section of Pacific closer to Sansome was the notorious Barbary Coast, where gangs and crime were rampant.

▲ Continue to Broadway. At the corner of Montgomery is the On Lok organization's Senior Health Services Center, which includes 35 apartments for low-income elderly. Seniors are brought by van and stay for the day to receive health and personal care and the midday meal. They participate in social and recreation activities and are returned home in the evening. One of the exciting programs is the ongoing, intergenerational garden shared by the frail elderly and about 24 children, ages two to five, from the Child Care program. The garden, transformed from an abandoned cement playground by the San Francisco League of Urban Gardeners, was additionally funded by several groups, among them San Francisco Beautiful.

▲ Turn left on Broadway to Kearny, then right to ascend the sidewalk stairway to Vallejo. Each time I walk here I expect the Edwardian homes on the odd-numbered side to be gone, and apartments or condos to have taken their place. Underneath the street paving you can see remains of the former cobblestone surface.

▲ Turn right on Vallejo. As you reach higher ground, look back to see the structures built on the edge of Yerba Buena Cove—the Pyramid, the Bank of California, and the Tishman Bldg.

▲ Looking west you see Russian Hill and the stairway leading up to the Vallejo Terrace (Walk 4). As you walk east, you come to the house at No. 448-B Vallejo. It was here that Madame Luisa Tetrazzini (1871–1940), the famous Italian opera soprano, while out walking (she was on tour in San Francisco) heard the young—12 or 13 years of age—Lena Pagliughi (born 1910), singing. Tetrazzini told Lena's parents she wanted to take their daughter to Italy to teach her opera and help launch her career as the second Madame Tetrazzini. The parents refused, but four years later, Lena did travel to Italy to begin her vocal studies under the direction of Tetrazzini. She subsequently had a long career with the Metropolitan Opera.

▲ Walk down the Vallejo Stairway, designed by the Department of Public Works. The Department of Urban Forestry planted the trees and shrubs and maintains them. Neighbors have planted additional flowers. Some residents in their 70s and 80s who live adjacent to the stairway attribute their longevity to daily stairway walking.

▲ Turn left on Montgomery to ascend the stairway to Union. Turn right into the Union cul-de-sac, then right into Calhoun. Some of the oldest houses in San Francisco are in this block. Nos. 291, 291-A, and 287 were built in the 1860s. The high retaining wall at the end of the street was built by the Works Progress Administration in 1939.

▲ Return to Montgomery and turn right. We stop for a moment in the middle of the street to look at No. 1360. The exterior is in the shape of a ship, complete with a ship-like upper deck. Etched into the glass over the central entrance are a gazelle, palm trees, and ocean waves. The graffiti panels on the side of the Art Moderne apartment house show The Worker holding the globe of the world above the Bay Bridge. The actual Bay Bridge towers just beyond it repeat the bridge towers on the panel. What extraordinary planning! It trumps trompe l'oeil. Actually, the apartment house is more famous as the setting for the 1947 movie, *Dark Passage*, which starred Humphrey Bogart and Lauren Bacall.

▲ Before descending the historic Filbert Stairway on the left side of No. 1360, note the well-designed garden with trees planted along the retaining wall of lower Montgomery. About midway along the wall is the humorous mural of Ginger, an apricot-colored teacup poodle. Dick Fosselman and Rick Helf, the artists, cleverly incorporated the actual water hydrant into the scene. The garden and the mural compose yet another of the surprise beauty spots we'll discover in the neighborhoods.

▲ A plaque on the Filbert Stairway says: FILBERT STEPS, DARRELL PLACE, NAPIER LANE. IN APPRECIATION OF GRACE MARCHANT FOR UNSELFISH, DEVOTED ENERGY IN THE BEAUTIFICATION OF FILBERT GARDENS. The late Grace Marchant moved to the Filbert Stairway in 1950, when the area was a dumping ground 30 feet deep. The city gave her permission to burn the dump; it burned for three days. For 30 years she labored on the stairway gardens, which were dedicated to her on May 4, 1980. Marchant died in 1982 at the age of 96. Her neighbor, friend, and protégé, Gary Kray, cares for the gardens. The city contributes water for their maintenance.

▲ Darrell Pl. and Napier Ln. are "paper streets." Although they appear as streets on maps and in street guides, Darrell is more like a trail, while Napier consists only of 12-foot wooden planks. Filbert is a wooden stairway threading alongside the garden. Because fire is always a hazard in these areas where there is no room for trucks, the Fire Department stores equipment as inconspicuously as possible.

Next to the blue fire hydrants on the walkway (blue is the code for connection to a high-pressure system) is a storage box for two small fire hydrants and a hose. An undulating walkway planted with rose-bushes leads to No. 273 Filbert; the earliest request for water hookup for No. 267 was in January 1873. The Gothic cottage at No. 228 (1873) was once a grocery. Next door, No. 226, is a renovated miner's shack from 1863.

▶ The lower part of Filbert Stairway is concrete. Much of the over-growth of nasturtiums, fennel, and blackberries growing along the sides of the hill have been cut down. The design of the patterned aggregate Levi's Plaza across the street pulls us forward as we descend to Sansome. The landscaping by Lawrence Halprin Associates includes granite and trees to evoke the Sierra, where Levi Strauss began his career in 1851. Strauss supplied miners with heavy duck cloth pants, reinforced with copper rivets, to withstand the pulling and the tearing from tools. The cloth was serge *de Nîmes* (from Nîmes), France—hence, denim.

▶ Cross Sansome and turn right to walk on the sidewalk. As we stroll, we become aware of the craggy east slope of Telegraph Hill and the extraordinary plantings there—the efforts of two neighbors who rap-pelled down the hill to do the work. In spring, the hillside near Green is ablaze with color from Mexican primroses, poppies, and other flowers. Echium grows at the edge of the hill along the street.

▶ Turn right on Washington to Grant. On the right side of Grant, at No. 823, is a plaque commemorating the first tent dwelling in Yerba Buena, which was put up in June 1835 by William Richardson, an Englishman who had deserted the English whaler, *Orion*, 13 years before. Industrious and helpful to the community, Richardson mar-ried the commandant's daughter and became a naturalized citizen. The plaque is on the wall on the right side of the door. The display of purses from the adjoining store partially covered it when I was there, but I gently brushed them aside to reveal it.

▶ Turn left on Grant to California. At the northeast corner is Old St. Mary's, the first Catholic cathedral in San Francisco, dedicated in 1854. It was rebuilt after being damaged in the 1906 earthquake. Still an active parish, Old St. Mary's presents a fine noon concert series and an outreach program. You turn left on California, then right on Leidesdorff, then left on Pine. Walking toward Sansome, you can see the 1930 Pacific Exchange at No. 301 Pine, and the Ralph Stackpole sculpture that reflects the massiveness of the building (Miller and Pflueger). One of my favorite clocks in the City is on the Furth Bldg. at the northwest corner of Sansome. It is flanked by a lion on the left and a unicorn on the right.

▲ Turn right on Sansome to Market; then turn left on Market to 1st and your beginning.

Old

TELEGRAPH HILL & NORTH BEACH

Neighborhoods

You begin the walk in an historic area of North Beach—at the intersection of Mason and Bay. During the Gold Rush days, North Beach extended only to Francisco St., near the water line. Henry Meiggs, a New York lumberman, built one of the first wharfs into the Bay (between Mason and Powell), built a sawmill, and established a thriving lumber trade (with imports from Oregon). He was genial, well liked, and a cofounder of the San Francisco Philharmonic Society. He knew politicians and power brokers. He invested heavily in real estate in North Beach and neighborhoods farther west, believing that the area would develop rapidly. He was wrong. Meiggs found himself in the untenable position of being personally bankrupt, and, since he had embezzled City funds, responsible for a financial crisis in San Francisco. Banks closed, many permanently, and investors lost their savings. In 1854, "Honest Harry" Meiggs managed to sail away to Chile; he made another fortune building a railroad through the mountains to Peru. Though he repaid most of his San Francisco debts, he died in Lima in 1877, having been denied return to California.

During the 1850s, the North Beach waterfront was a dynamic community. Conditions were in flux: there were so many people coming in, both emigrants from the east and immigrants from overseas. Some were in transit, but others came to settle here. Supportive services were established—the fishing boats, the breweries, the forges, the slaughterhouses; there were restaurants and saloons, import stores, and hostelries.

The 1906 earthquake leveled everything in this quarter except the Ferry Building, which at that time was the tallest structure in San Francisco. The area was soon rebuilt, and the City celebrated its rebirth with the Panama-Pacific International Exposition of 1915.

Over the years the San Francisco port has diminished in importance. The thrust of the Port Authority's master plan is to balance maritime needs and the needs of the public. One of the plans for Fisherman's Wharf is to centralize the fish wholesalers in one facility, and return the

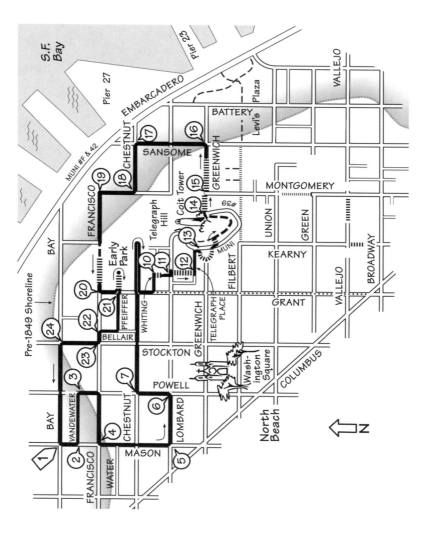

area to its original purpose—catching, preparing, and selling fish to residents and tourists alike.

Along the Embarcadero, the Pier 7 Esplanade is a popular site for walking, fishing, and picnicking; piers 80–96 are the container terminals.

WALK 2: Telegraph Hill & North Beach Route

Public Transportation: Cable Car to Bay and Taylor, walk one block; Muni Bus #39 to Bay and Mason; #30 to Bay and Leavenworth, walk three blocks.

1. Begin at Mason and Bay. South on Mason.
2. Left on Vandewater.
3. Right on Powell. Right on Francisco.
4. Left on Mason to Lombard.
5. Left on Lombard to Powell.
6. Left on Powell to Chestnut.
7. Right on Chestnut to the end of the street. Return to Grant, next to No. 1834.
8. Left on Grant to Whiting.
9. Left on Whiting St.
10. Right, across from No. 3, ascend Julius St. Stwy.
11. Walk to Lombard. Next to No. 363, ascend Stwy. to Telegraph Pl.
12. Left on Telegraph Pl. to Telegraph Hill Blvd. (for one-half block to see the whimsical sculpture on the roof).
13. Right on Telegraph Hill Blvd. Two doors away from No. 201 descend Stwy. into cul-de-sac of Greenwich (400 block). Walk around the planted area to the left; ascend stairway to Telegraph Hill Blvd. Cross Blvd to ascend the stone stairway up the hill toward Coit Tower. Follow the footpath that veers to the left and then toward the right side of the Tower.
14. Go around to the front of the Tower, then bear right to cross the Blvd. and descend the Greenwich Stwy. to Montgomery.
15. Cross Montgomery. Go right on lower Montgomery. Next to No.1460, descend to continue down Greenwich Stwy.
16. Left on Sansome to Chestnut.
17. Left on Chestnut to Montgomery.
18. Right on Montgomery to Francisco.
19. Left on Francisco. Ascend Stwy. to Francisco cul-de-sac and Grant.
20. Left on Grant to ascend Stwy. to Jack Early Park on left side of street.
21. Return to Grant and cross the street to walk through Pfeiffer St. to Bellair Pl. to Francisco.
22. Left on Francisco to Stockton.
23. Right on Stockton to Bay.
24. Left on Bay to Mason and your beginning.

▶ From the intersection of Mason and Bay, you walk south on Mason, and turn left on Vandewater St., a charming "twitton" as the British call it, softened by trees and housing many architect and designer offices in the low four-story buildings. Go to the end and turn right on Powell, and right on Francisco to see the Historical Site at No. 407. Until 1980, this was the Bauer-Schweitzer Malt Company, the last barrel-malting factory west of the Mississippi. Their high-quality malt was sold to small American breweries such as Anchor, and was also exported to Japan. When it became economically unfeasible to continue operations, the building was sold. It is currently being renovated for 88 condominiums to be completed in April 2001.

▶ Turn left on Mason. A mural of aquatic life embellishes the gymnasium wall adjoining the Joe DiMaggio Playground and pool. It's scheduled for a $6 million renovation. No. 660, the Telegraph Hill Neighborhood Center, was founded in 1890 by two wealthy women (influenced by Jane Addams of Hull House in Chicago) to provide services to immigrants from Europe. The program now includes health and educational services to new immigrants from the Pacific Rim, to seniors and children (both pre-school age and older). Flower beds provide an inviting entrance to the Center. The vegetable garden is in the back.

▶ One of the most abundant displays of cascading, fuchsia-colored bougainvillea in the City adorns No. 604 Lombard. The vine was planted in 1938; it blooms twice a year, and each year it seems to become more exuberant. The contrast of its color with the six junipers (their shapes suggest ladybugs) planted along the wall of the apartment house is an additional reward.

▶ Turn left on Powell and right on Chestnut. Two blocks down, at the intersection of Grant and Chestnut, you have a long view of Marin toward the north and west. Besides the boats anchored at Fisherman's Wharf, you can see Piers 33 and 35 and perhaps a container ship proceeding toward the Oakland port. More distant is Pier 39, well known for its fine horticultural displays of container-flowers; for a colony of sea lions that have taken up residence along the wharf; for good restaurants and friendly stores. The outdoor spaces encourage strolling, and the area is very popular with young people and children. It's a great place to watch fireworks on July 4. (These are important enough reasons to lessen my negative reaction to the architecture.) Angel Island State Park is to the north.

- No. 298 Chestnut is a Mediterranean-style home built in 1929. Its tile roof, marble entry, and ceramic Della Robbia plaque are visible through the iron gates. Walk to the end of the cul-de-sac along the left side (designated as Open Space) to obtain a view of the "lowlands," and return to Grant.

- At Grant turn left (south) and left again into Whiting cul-de-sac. Three fourths into the block and to the right, ascend the nine steps of Julius Alley Stairway and walk to the end, which brings you to Lombard Street. To the left of No. 363 is the short Child St. Stairway. Walk up to Telegraph Pl. and turn left (No. 69 is a Japanese-inspired home) to Telegraph Hill Blvd. Turn left for one-half block to see some unusual, whimsical sculptures on the roof. The oversized spectacles that regard the people looking at the spectacles seem perfectly normal, and the copper camel and its rider seem perfectly at home by the water. After a few minutes I realize size and object and setting are not normal. Then I laugh and decide we need more sculptures to surprise us. Albert Guibata is the artist.

- Turn right. Next to No. 201, descend a stairway into the Greenwich St. cul-de-sac. Circle around the oval garden area a neighboring homeowner planted (except for the trees) and maintains. Walk up the opposite stairway to Telegraph Hill Blvd.

- Cross the Blvd. to ascend the stone stairway leading to the top of Telegraph Hill. In the early days it was known as Signal Hill, because from here ships' arrivals would be signaled across the City. In the 1880s, a restaurant was the chief attraction on the hill.

- Bear right on the footpath that goes toward and around the back of Coit Tower, veering to the left, and then right. Coit Tower, a universally recognized icon of the city, was designed by architect Arthur Brown Jr. (City Hall) and dedicated in 1933 to the Knickerbocker Engine Company No. 5, one of San Francisco's volunteer fire-fighting companies. It was funded by Lillie Hitchcock Coit, who, as a small child, loved to follow No. 5 and became their mascot. The tower rises 179 feet from the crest of Telegraph Hill, itself 284 feet high.

- Turn right on the redwood-bark path and sit down on the bench for a view of the graceful 1895 Ferry Building and its famous clock: lit at night, it is a cameo—a Cinderella—surpassing all other commercial buildings in its delicate beauty. Arthur Brown Jr.'s original landscape design for the area around Coit Tower will be completed in 2001–2002, thanks to a dedicated pro-bono group, the Pioneer Park

Greenwich Street

Project, who have raised the money for the construction of three new stairways leading to Coit Tower, a picnic area overlooking the Bay, a wheelchair-accessible ramp, and native plants and trees.

▲ The tall, slender Embarcadero buildings to the southeast are on the site of the old wholesale produce market. Because Embarcadero Center is on redevelopment land and Federal funds partially defrayed building costs, the developer was obliged to spend 1% of the total project cost on art works. The result has been excellent sculpture located throughout the Center. Directly in front of you is the Transamerica Pyramid, built on the original shoreline (Walk 1). The 48-story dark carnelian granite structure is the Bank of America Building on California.

▲ As you walk along the right side of Coit Tower, look inside and see the WPA murals executed in the 1930s. Intermittent vandalism and/or damage from water seepage have necessitated closing the mural rooms to visitors from time to time. The elevator ride to the top floor is available to the public at a nominal charge. The parking lot has coin telescopes to bring Marin and the East Bay into close-up view.

▲ Walk down the front stairs of the Tower, take the footpath to the right, and cross Telegraph Hill Blvd. to descend the Greenwich Stairway. The upper brick section of the stairway curves, allowing room on each side for wide, terraced, private gardens. The lane running at right angles from No. 356 Greenwich has no name. It connects with the Filbert Stairway farther south (Walk 1).

▲ The first landing of these 147 stairs leads down to the Montgomery cul-de-sac and the famous Julius' Castle restaurant, built in 1923. A beautiful, mature fig tree graces the entrance. Because the lower retaining wall was designed in a random pattern of brick with protruding stones, which is extremely photogenic, I always look back before descending the next set of stairs.

▲ Cross Montgomery (you may feel like an opera singer taking a deep breath) and bear right to the Greenwich sign. Descend the concrete stairs and extended walkways. Along the way you see a cistern for fire fighting, and, on the left side of the walkway, trees (a magnificent magnolia) and gardens (roses and irises, ferns and fuchsias). The resident flock of wild parrots obtains sustenance from juniper berries and loquats near No. 243. A mature princess tree dominates the garden across from No. 237.

- A tall Deodar cedar and a redwood in the canyon provide homes for families of birds. Nasturtiums and invasive fennel usually line the hillsides. In season, blackberries can be picked. At the foot of the steps, turn left on Sansome and continue north.

- The slope of Telegraph Hill, now barely seen from Sansome and Lombard since the Lombard Plaza apartments were built in 1991, was the amphitheater for the 1966 Janice Joplin rock concert.

- Turn left on Chestnut. A three-story brick structure (originally built in the late 1800s, reconstructed in 1973) is angled across the corner of Montgomery. You turn right on Montgomery and left on Francisco.

- At the cross street of Kearny walk into the well-cared-for courtyard of the Wharf Plaza subsidized housing for seniors. The gardens are a pleasant place for the residents to sit and visit, and in September the area is spectacular with gingko trees ringed in gold leaves. Ascend the well-designed stairway. It features an unusual, long, elevated walkway—perfect for a stairway dance performance. At the top of the stairway you reach the Francisco cul-de-sac. The Telegraph Terrace condos fit snugly into the block and around the corner onto Grant.

- Turn left on Grant. In the middle of the block, make another left to walk up the stairs to Jack Early Park. Beginning in 1962 Jack Early ("Mr. Tree"), in a one-man effort, started planting trees and flowers in a neglected area. He remembered carrying water buckets by hand from his house on Pfeiffer. Now Telegraph Terrace Association maintains the Park. It is a rewarding place for views, solitude, and moon-watching.

- Come back down the stairway, cross Grant, and walk through Pfeiffer Alley, a right-of-way that has become a special enclave. No. 139–141 dates from 1910, and No. 152 from 1891.

- Turn right into Bellair Pl. New paving stones and recessed spaces for plants are welcoming tokens of promise. Make a left on Francisco and cross the street to see the little cottage at No. 276, which dates from 1863. Delicious aromas emanate from No. 271, now a cooking school.

- Continue west on Francisco to Stockton. Turn right to Bay, and left to your beginning.

You have explored some of the alleyways and lanes and right-of-ways that are plentiful in North Beach. If you want to explore the neighborhood shopping areas on Columbus or upper Grant, you will find lots of foot traffic, small shops, restaurants, and coffee houses with outdoor tables and chairs. Many of the old Italian businesses have closed; Chinese signs are common on stores.

Those who have lived in the City for years are nostalgic about the old North Beach. Columbus Day (in fall) and the Blessing of the Fishing Fleet (in spring) were first celebrated in North Beach. Small opera houses on Green, Stockton, and Columbus were very well attended. Once only Italian vaudeville was performed at the Flag St. Theater at Stockton and Columbus. Tom Cara introduced the espresso machine from Italy after World War II. Enrico Banducci introduced new entertainers at his *hungry i* club, who included Barbra Streisand, Woody Allen, and the

Telegraph Hill—circa 1880

photographer unknown

Kingston Trio. Comedians Lenny Bruce and Phyllis Diller first appeared at the Purple Onion on Columbus. At one time 12 accordion makers were doing a lively business in North Beach. (In 1990 the Court of Historical Review decided that the accordion was the official instrument of San Francisco.) The Beat poets held readings in the coffee houses on upper Grant during the 1950s; Lawrence Ferlinghetti's City Lights Bookstore still continues from those days (No. 261 Columbus). The zany revue, Beach Blanket Babylon, has been performing continuously since 1974.

To learn more about the neighborhood, visit the North Beach Museum at 1435 Stockton, above Eureka Federal Savings, which is open to the public free-of-charge. Washington Square, the piazza on Stockton between Union and Filbert (now City Landmark No. 226), was reserved as a park in the City plan of 1847. It was one of the City parks that sheltered the 1906 earthquake homeless in prefabricated camp cottages. Fragments of memories that people have shared over the years compose the ambiance of North Beach. First-time visitors will not share this background, but the abundance of specialty stores at street level, the number of eating places, the general friendliness, and the density of neighborhood foot traffic invite further exploring.

Phyllis Pearsall (1906–1996), the founder of Geographer's A–Z Map Company, walked for 18 hours daily, beginning at 5:00 a.m., to list 23,000 roads in London. Asked if she got lost in London, she replied, "Always, dear." She walked 3000 miles.

Further Ambling

If you'd like to shop for food or sundry items, you have choices available in all directions, within comfortable walking distances. You could walk south on Grant into the upper Grant area and Columbus. Many Asian restaurants plus the poultry and fish and vegetable markets of Chinatown are one block west, on Stockton. The Cost Plus import store at No. 2552 Taylor is a popular place to buy inexpensive, imported trinkets, foods, and housewares. The Cannery, six blocks west at the foot of Columbus, at No. 2801 Leavenworth, is an unusual shopping complex; Ghirardelli Square, two blocks beyond, is another historic setting for specialty shops (Walk 6).

Castles in

the Air

Nob Hill, 376 feet above the Bay, is wedged
between Pacific Heights to the west, Russian Hill
toward the north, and North Beach and Chinatown
to the east. Millions of tourists have traversed Nob Hill
on the cable cars, gliding both north-south on Powell St.
between Market St. and Fisherman's Wharf, and east-west on
California St. (the Powell St. line began operations in 1887; the
California St. cable railway began in 1878).

A paradox of this walk is that the most interesting characteristics
can be noted by standing still—looking up to make out the lofty architectural details on the buildings and looking from eye level to register
the delight of cable car riders. Binoculars add extended range to your
sightings.

Nob Hill is famous for the views, luxury hotels, and apartment
houses that you can see on the walk. The only "neighbors" in this section may be doormen, or hotel guests alighting from a taxi, or the elderly rich assisted by nurses or companions. But there is a neighborhood,
and in the side streets and alleyways there are "talking" neighbors to
visit with, and gardening neighbors who might share cuttings. The Nob
Hill Association, the neighborhood watchdog organization founded in
1923, is actively concerned with the environment and community issues.

▶ You begin the walk at California and Leavenworth on the crest of
Nob Hill. Walk north on Leavenworth, along the odd-numbered side
for a few yards, and turn left into Acorn, one of San Francisco's

attractive, viable alleys, full of plants and color. The inviting green walkway, green pots full of flowers ringed around an utility pole, plus bedding plants and raised beds of flowers, is the work of neighbors who have cared for the alley for many years. (Note the Dutch oven, now painted green, which is used as a flowerpot.)

▶ From Acorn, turn north on Leavenworth toward Sacramento St. Dashiell Hammett lived in the brick and stucco building on the corner at No. 1155 while he finished *The Maltese Falcon*. Chicos grocery at No. 1168 was famous for its excellent produce. It was in the same family from 1928 to 1997. The two Chicos cousins (both named Sam) became partners when their fathers retired. They continued the deliveries and special services throughout the Nob Hill neighborhood: buying items for their customers that they did not regularly stock, driving a customer to the hospital in their truck, and taking care of their customers' apartment keys. Residents still talk about the Sams with warmth and affection. Their grocery was a Nob Hill institution.

▶ The No. 27 Muni stops in front of the store. Cross Sacramento St. to see the corner building with two addresses, Nos. 1202–1206 Leavenworth and Nos. 1380–1390 Sacramento. Designed by Julia Morgan in 1910, it is a Craftsman-style shingle structure. Turn right on Sacramento and walk on the odd-numbered side. The foliage of evenly spaced ficus street trees adds a softness that makes this section of Sacramento St. inviting.

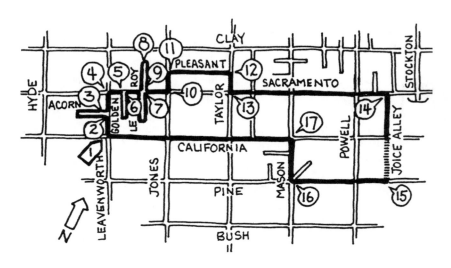

▶ Turn right into Golden Ct. (the name GOLDEN is on the upper side of the first house). Shrubs of yellow, white, and orange datura are planted on both sides of the walkway. The owner built the gray asbestos-sided house on our right in 1950 (the address is officially No. 1154 Leavenworth) on the only empty lot on the street. He planted the *tiglio* (known in the U.S. as the linden) tree in 1947 from a seedling his mother brought in her purse from Italy. Golden Ct. is especially photogenic.

▶ Leroy Alley, our next right turn off Sacramento, has two symmetrical rows of ficus trees that frame the walk/cul-de-sac. No. 16 Leroy has attractive bowed windows. Go across Sacramento into the continuation of Leroy. Tall bottlebrush trees on one side and ficus trees on the other enhance the short alley. A basilica-shaped structure at the end of the street is the back of No. 1239 Jones St., the Tank High Pressure System of the Fire Department.

▶ We walk out of the cul-de-sac and make a left turn on Sacramento. No. 1315–1325 is a six-flat Edwardian. Continue to Jones.

▶ Grace Episcopal Cathedral School for Boys is on the lower level of the corner of the square block that includes the Diocesan house and the Cathedral itself. You can see the brightly colored playground

WALK 3: Nob Hill Route

Public Transportation: Leavenworth is on the route of Muni Bus #27; Sacramento and Clay Sts. are on the #1 California St. trolley bus. California Cable Car Line runs on California.

1. Begin at California and Leavenworth. North on Leavenworth to Acorn.
2. Left on Acorn. Return to Leavenworth.
3. Left on Leavenworth to Sacramento.
4. Right on Sacramento to Golden.
5. Right on Golden. Return to Sacramento.
6. Right on Sacramento to Leroy.
7. Right on Leroy. Return to Sacramento.
8. Left on Leroy. Return to Sacramento.
9. Left on Sacramento to Jones.
10. Left on Jones to Pleasant.
11. Right on Pleasant to Taylor.
12. Right on Taylor to Sacramento.
13. Left on Sacramento to Joice.
14. Right on Joice Alley; descend Stwy. to Pine.
15. Right on Pine to Mason.
16. Right on Mason to California.
17. Left on California to your beginning.

equipment. The school was built in 1966 for grades kindergarten through eighth. Turn left on Jones.

▶ The 1200 and 1300 blocks feature luxury apartments and restaurants: No.1221 Jones, Le Club at No.1250, the Comstock Apartments at No.1333. Next to No.1234, turn right into Pleasant Alley. The sidewalk and street are traditionally clean of debris. The metrocedros trees are newly planted. No.75 Pleasant has extravagantly large north-facing windows. Across the street is the back of a concrete parking garage. A brass plate on the door of No. 40–44 admonishes, NO SMOKING.

▶ Make a right turn (south) on Taylor. Across the street at No. 1110 is the smallest structure on the block, a one-story, modified, three-window bay, originally built by James Flood for his coachman.

▶ Turn left on Sacramento. No. 1182 has a mailbox at about sidewalk level and a plaque next to it commemorating its Nob Hill architectural award for excellence in 1960. In the sidewalk in front of No. 1162 Sacramento is a survey monument with the precise latitude and longitude of this spot inscribed under its cover.

▶ The widow of Collis P. Huntington, one of the Big Four railroad barons, donated Huntington Park across the street to the City in 1915. The Huntington home on the property was demolished by the 1906 quake. The Park is well designed for various activities by adults and children. The northern section has swings, slides, and a large sandbox. The middle and southern section feature the Fountain of the Turtles, a delight to contemplate while sitting on the comfortable bench. The Nob Hill Association, in conjunction with Friends of Recreation and Parks, financed a recent renovation of the park, and has undertaken the responsibility for maintaining it.

▶ As you walk along, the back of the landmark Pacific Union Club, one of the most exclusive men's clubs in the country, comes into view. James Flood, of the Comstock silver mines, built this brownstone building as his residence in 1886. Its exterior survived the quake and fire of 1906. Willis Polk reconstructed and remodeled the home in 1912. The legend that has trickled down through the generations (which we all like to believe, not much caring if it's fact or fiction) says that Flood hired a full-time maintenance man to keep the bronze fence around the property polished.

▶ Look at the white granite Fairmont Hotel. It was readied for its grand opening in 1906. On April 18 at 5:15 a.m., the fire caused by the earthquake destroyed the interior. Luckily, the fire insurance didn't expire until midnight! The steel frame survived, and a year later the hotel opened for business. A contemporary feature of the Fairmont is the exterior elevator, providing an unusual kinetic experience as you gradually ascend while watching the cityscape.

▶ Continue east on Sacramento. You can see cars crossing the Bay Bridge through the narrow opening between skyscrapers. No. 1000 Mason is the elegant Brocklebank Apartments, built in 1924. Ornate mythological beasts are positioned atop the entrance (Hitchcock's movie *Vertigo* was filmed here).

▶ The Donaldina Cameron House is down the hill at No. 920 Sacramento. It was formerly the Chinese Presbyterian Mission Home. The Mission began efforts in 1874 to rescue young Chinese girls brought to San Francisco as factory slaves and prostitutes. Ms. Cameron joined the group in 1895 and continued her missionary work for 40 years. Cameron House currently provides community recreational and social services. The clinker-brick structure was built in 1881, and then rebuilt in 1907 by Julia Morgan. Morgan worked in the Bay Area from about 1905 to the 1930s, designing Craftsman-style homes and also elegant structures such as the Hearst Castle at San Simeon.

▶ Cross Sacramento and walk into Joice Alley. Continue in the right-of-way and cross California St. Ahead at No. 845 is an Art Deco, a pleasingly symmetrical apartment house with a marble entrance and elaborate light fixtures. If you look to the right, you can see the octagonal green-and-white, electronically operated traffic-control tower for the cable car system at California and Powell. Continue on Joice to the stairway and descend. Two magnolia trees are planted at the first landing. A small shrine to St. Francis is on the lower landing near the graceful curve of the stairs at Pine. The flats, Nos. 738, 740, and 742 Pine are built in the Pueblo style. Across the street is Monroe Alley, now renamed Dashiell Hammett St. Hammett fans may want to detour to Bush St. and go into Burritt Alley (between Stockton and Powell) to see the bronze plaque.

▶ Turn right on Pine. At the corner, above the high parapet in back of the Stanford Court Hotel, is a cast-stone penguin by Beniamino Bufano, the impecunious artist and bohemian who captured the imagination of San Franciscans and, more importantly, the financial support of patrons. At the time of his death in 1970, many of his works were stored in warehouses. Others are scattered in several places: in the courtyard of the Academy of Sciences; in the North Terminal of the Airport; at the Phelan St. entrance to the Administration Building of San Francisco City College; in the meadow at Ft. Mason (Walk 6), at The Mansion Hotel, and in the Ordway Building lobby in Oakland.

▲ You are now walking along the original granite retaining wall of the Stanford mansion, which was destroyed by the earthquake. The blocked entrance in the wall may have been for tradesmen. The tower with the finial marks the division between the Stanford and Hopkins properties.

▲ Turn right on Mason and walk uphill on the even-numbered side. A graduated series of town houses, Nos. 831–849, designed by Willis Polk around 1918, provides an imaginative counterfoil to the sumptuous structures on the hill.

> *Louis Montesquieu (born 1689)—When he arrived in a new town, he liked to climb up a high tower and get a good overall look at the place, then come down and examine the different parts at leisure.*

▲ As your bird's-eye view from the top—California St. between Mason and Taylor—comes into focus, you see lines of formidable structures: the Fairmont, Mark Hopkins, and Huntington hotels; and the Pacific Union Club. The Stanford Court Hotel anchors the Powell St. side; Grace Cathedral and the Cathedral Apartments are on the Jones St. side. The secondary line along Sacramento St. consists of luxury apartments.

▲ Standing on the summit, and looking at the details of the Mark Hopkins Hotel and the Fairmont Hotel across the street, you can't help "seeing" the street as it was in the late 1870s and 1880s, before it was destroyed by the 1906 earthquake and fire. Owners of the Central Pacific Railroad and the Comstock silver mine built the ornate, grandiose homes of one of the most elaborate streets in the country.

▲ Turn left on California. No. 1001, The Morsehead apartment building (1915), is one of my favorites on the hill. Behind the terra-cotta columns and facade are 10 apartments, each 2000 to 3000 square feet. The building feels cozier than many on the block. Another favorite Nob Hill building is No. 1021, a single-family dwelling, with ornate wrought-iron double doors, French doors on the second story, and cut-lace coverings on the windows and glass doors. No. 1075 California is the Huntington Hotel, considered by many to be one of the most elegant hotels in the City.

- You are passing the California St. entrance to Huntington Park. From the Taylor St. side of the park, you face the rose-window facade of Grace Cathedral. The 1993 $11 million construction project completed the design as envisioned by the original architect, Lewis Hobart. The Great Stairway entrance, extending up from Taylor St., permits a full view of the magnificent, cast-bronze doors (made from the molds of the Renaissance sculptor, Lorenzo Ghiberti). At the top is a wide plaza and promenade, and the labyrinth, based on the one at Chartres Cathedral, a tool for meditative walking.

- The cornerstone of Grace Cathedral was laid in 1910; the exterior was completed in 1964. Samuel Yellin executed the subdued, elegant, wrought-ironwork on the gates to the Chapel of Grace, on the south side nearest the California St. entrance. Murals by Antonio Sotomayor, chronicling Cathedral and Parish history, are inside the chapel.

- Concerts—sacred, secular, organ, choral, or jazz—are regularly presented. Acoustics are excellent. Duke Ellington was commissioned by the Diocese to compose a sacred piece, which was performed at a concert in 1965. During the Christmas season of 1990, Bobby McFerrin, the San Francisco singer and conductor, organized a 24-hour sing-a-thon "healing," with various musical groups participating.

- The Crocker family donated the land to the Diocese on which the Cathedral complex stands. Charles Crocker was the fourth of the Big Four railroad kings, and the fact that there is now a religious institution on his property is an irony to savor. In retaliation for being denied the adjoining lot to complete his purchase of the square block, Crocker put up a 40-foot-high "spite fence," which cut off the sun and view from Nicholas Yung's house at 1203 Sacramento at Taylor. Crocker's heirs finally bought Yung's property from his estate.

- Now continue west on California to Leavenworth, to arrive at your beginning.

Speaking of

Intangibles

Every San Francisco neighborhood has its unique ambiance—a distillation of the folklore and stories of its early days surviving through its continual modifications. Russian Hill acquired its name from an early cemetery located on the east side of Vallejo and Jones where Russian sailors were buried before the Gold Rush (a stairway is located on the site). Greek Orthodox crosses and bones were unearthed there. The sailors had probably come down from Fort Ross, the Russian settlement, with the pelts of seals and otters. In the late 1800s—and especially after the 1906 earthquake demolished other structures—small cottages expressing the special ambiance of the neighborhood adorned Russian Hill. The active Russian Hill Neighbors Association is working diligently to preserve this sense of neighborhood in the face of great economic and demographic changes. They are fighting the demolition of cottages and their replacement with three and four-story condominiums. Only about 40 cottages remain out of 100 originally built.

Russian Hill is a craggy, physically compact area. Jasper O'Farrell, the City surveyor, in 1847 extended the street grid to Leavenworth. Somehow, working theoretically and on paper, he didn't make allowance for the hills. As a result of the rectangular street configuration, the summit of Russian Hill became isolated. At Jones Street a ladder was placed against the bluff to access the 1000 block of Vallejo. Broadway, Vallejo, and Green were impassable for horse teams. These features attracted people who desired a measure of independence with proximity to the City center. The hilltop housing sites made possible the magnificent views, which are still a reason to live on Russian Hill. The topography also encouraged a sense of community among residents. For many years, a large coterie of writers including Bret Harte, George Sterling, and Ina Coolbrith resided on the hill.

- ▶ You begin at Filbert and Polk, and walk east (uphill) on the 1300 block of Filbert. Homes barely visible from the sidewalk are tucked in along this block. No. 1364 has an orchard, and No. 1338 has a wooden stake fence, gardens, and a long brick walk shared with ten apartment cottages.

- ▶ The 1200 block of Filbert, from Larkin to Hyde, is composed mostly of Edwardian flats with bay windows on the two upper stories. The block has few trees, but next to No. 1252 is a terraced rock garden. The angled stairway at No. 1234 with its landings appears like a hopscotch diagram. The brown-shingled building at the corner is designed in the Craftsman style. There are more "tuck-ins" across the street.

- ▶ Continue past the hum of cables in the slot of Hyde St., to walk down the Filbert (sidewalk) Stairway. At the bottom of the hill turn right on Leavenworth. A half block away, next to 2033 Leavenworth, you ascend Havens Stairway, a little-known stairway that can only be accessed from Leavenworth (it formerly continued through to Hyde).

- ▶ The gardens alongside the stairway are cultivated by the property owners living on Havens. The fern garden is one of the most attractive additions to the green space. You can see Coit Tower and the Bay Bridge, as you return to Leavenworth.

- ▶ At Leavenworth turn right (south) toward Union. In the middle of the next block, next to No. 1934 Leavenworth, you turn left on Macondray Lane, one of Russian Hill's secluded pathway/stairways, and follow it to Taylor. This end of Macondray begins with an unattractive driveway/alley, followed by a narrow tree-lined sidewalk. After crossing Jones you walk through a trellised entry into an unexpected garden path, the magical part of Macondray. You see goldfish ponds, garden ornaments, and both annual and perennial plantings. The bordering condos are small but attractive. The area feels as though it ought to be private gardens, but Macondray Lane is a public right-of-way. It is the setting for Armistead Maupin's *Tales of The City*. The exposed sandstone outcrop, the various materials used for the stairway—wood, cobblestone, and brick, and the variety of trees and shrubs in every shade of green add to the appeal of Macondray Lane, named for a 19th Century merchant and viticulturist.

▲ Turn right on Taylor and walk to Green. Ascend the stairway to the cul-de-sac, passing an elaborate Art Moderne apartment house on

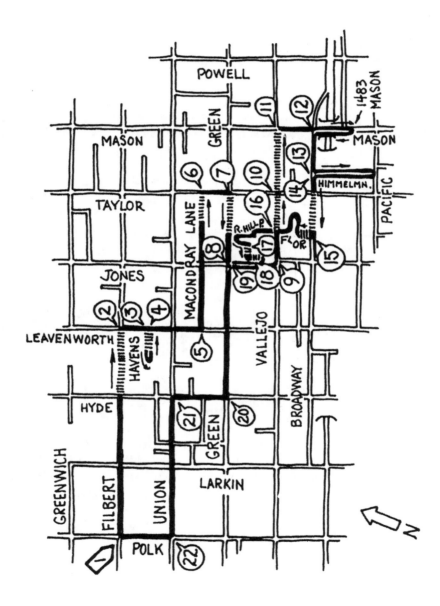

the left, and an inviting mauve-colored, wood-frame house from the 1890s.

▶ Towering above everything in sight is No. 999 Green, the Eichler Summit Apartments, built before the height-limitation law was passed in 1970. In the center of the tower, three, long, open, oval shapes like huge exclamation points appear to punctuate the end of a special block, the 1000 block of Green that escaped fire and earthquake damage in 1906.

▶ Walk to Jones and turn left to enter the arched, double-stairway entrance to a very special section of Vallejo. It is part of Russian Hill's Vallejo St. Crest District, which is on the National Register of Historic Places.

▶ You might call this the Livermore section of Vallejo. Since the 1850s, some member of the family has lived continuously in this enclave, staunchly supporting efforts to preserve and maintain the unique character and beauty of the area. You might also call it the

WALK 4: Russian Hill South Route

Public Transportation: Muni Bus #19 goes on Polk; Hyde St. Cable Car goes on Hyde—walk two blocks west to Polk.

1. Begin at Polk and Filbert. East on Filbert; descend sidewalk Stwy. to Leavenworth.
2. Right on Leavenworth.
3. Ascend Havens Stwy., and return to Leavenworth.
4. Right on Leavenworth.
5. Left into Macondray Lane.
6. Right on Taylor to Green.
7. Ascend Green Stwy. to Jones.
8. Left on Jones.
9. Left onto Vallejo Stwy. into cul-de-sac; walk to end.
10. Descend Vallejo Stwy. next to No. 1019, past Taylor to Mason.
11. Right on Mason. Cross Broadway to see No. 1483 Mason.
12. Cross back to Broadway; left (west) on Broadway.
13. Left to Himmelman Pl.
14. Return to Broadway; continue west on sidewalk Stwy. past Taylor to Florence.
15. Ascend Florence Stwy.
16. Walk across Vallejo into Russian Hill Pl.
17. Right to walk down ramp to Jones.
18. Right on Jones to Green.
19. Left on Green to Hyde.
20. Right on Hyde to Union.
21. Right on Polk to Filbert to your beginning.

Livermore/Polk section. The architect Willis Polk was hired by Horatio Livermore (and later by his son Norman) to build many of the houses and design both the entrance on Jones and the stairway to Taylor.

- Continue to the end of the cul-de-sac, walking on the odd-numbered south side. No. 1045 (originally No. 1023, now No. 40 Florence) was the original Horatio Livermore house, built in 1865. Willis Polk remodeled it, adding a top floor that permitted views in every direction. A developer demolished three redwood-shingled houses at No. 1030, designed by Joseph Worcester circa 1889. They have since been replaced by the Hermitage condominium apartments, which duplicate the Craftsman style so appropriate for the nooks and crannies of Russian Hill. The architects, Joseph Worcester, Julia Morgan, Bernard Maybeck, Willis Polk, and Ernest Coxhead built homes in this style during the first quarter of the 20th Century as an antidote to the excesses and formalism of Victorian architecture. They emphasized natural elements: redwood shingles, protruding eaves instead of bracketed cornices, and gabled roofs. Trees and shrubs were an important parts of the design, and homes were set into the property to blend harmoniously with the topography.

- Polk (1867–1924) designed No. 1019 for the artist Doris Williams (notice the high, half-moon window in her north-facing studio). As part of his fee, he was given the adjoining lot. Here he built No. 1013 for himself in 1892. The house drops down through six levels, and is now divided into three apartments.

- In 1915 Laura Ingalls Wilder, who wrote the *Little House on the Prairie* series, came to San Francisco to see the Panama-Pacific International Exposition. She stayed with her daughter, Rose, a feature writer for the *San Francisco Bulletin*, who lived at No. 1019. Laura wrote letters home to her husband in Missouri about the Fair, the City, the people, and life on the hill. These letters have been collected in a small paperback, *West From Home*.

Horatio Gates Livermore walked from St. Joseph, Missouri to San Francisco in 1850.

- The Open Space at the top of the hill was the 50-vara[1] lot that Horatio Livermore bought in 1889. In 1914, after the residents had

---

[1] According to *Merriam Webster's Collegiate Dictionary*, 10th ed., *vara* is "a Texas unit of length equal to 33.33 inches (84.66 centimeters)."

Vallejo Street

subscribed $25,000 for the balustrades and ramps that Polk designed on the Jones side, the top of the summit became the carriage turnaround.

▲ The story of the Polk-designed Vallejo Stairway, which you descend is one of concerted effort by neighbors over a period of many years to beautify and maintain the surrounding gardens. The neighbors have been generous in sharing with other neighborhood groups what they learned in organizing, maneuvering through City departments, and approaching non-governmental agencies for funding. (They are also the inspiration for the Los Angeles Los Feliz neighborhood major stairway and ceramic mural wall project.)

▲ Fifty neighbors have banded together as a division of the Russian Hill Neighbors Association to continue the beautification process. Fourteen lights, replicas of early lamps (now with halogen bulbs), have been installed and paid for by the neighbors. Cleanup days are well attended. Benches have been installed and seasonal plantings are ongoing. The area is a delight for every walker.

▲ Across from No. 1715 Taylor, you enter the Ina Donna Coolbrith Park (dedicated in 1911), to walk to Mason. Ina Coolbrith (1841–1928), whose uncle Joseph Smith founded the Mormon Church, came to San Francisco from Illinois at the age of 10 in the first covered-wagon train that crossed the Sierra via the Beckwourth Pass. She taught school and later became librarian at the Bohemian Club and the Oakland Public Library. Although she was honored as poet laureate of California in 1915, her main contribution to the San Francisco literary world was as a catalyst to aspiring writers. Joaquin Miller, George Sterling, Bret Harte, Gelett Burgess, and others met regularly at her home (1067 Broadway) for readings.

▲ Many elderly Chinese-Americans come to the park daily to practice Tai Chi. Their mental concentration and slow body movements echo the harmony conveyed by the surrounding canopy of Monterey pines.

▲ At Mason you're on the edge of Chinatown and Russian Hill. Turn right for one block, then right again on Broadway. Notice how the land dips and rises, extending to the highest point south, Nob Hill (Walk 3).

▲ You are now above the Broadway Tunnel, which extends under Russian Hill from Mason to Larkin. Although the tunnel was proposed in 1874 to facilitate the flow of traffic, it opened for vehicular traffic in 1952, 78 years later!

▶ Walk across Broadway to No. 1483 Mason to see the 69-unit Lady Shaw Center for senior housing, which was completed in late 1990. Building above the tunnel was a controversial issue, but the critical need for housing in Chinatown, the fine design by architect Gordon Chong & Associates, and the infusion of private, City, and Federal funding were decisive factors in favor of construction.

▶ Go back across the street, turn left on Broadway to look at the former twin-towered Spanish National Church, Nuestra Señora de Guadalupe, at No. 906. The 1912 structure built on the site of the original 1875 wooden church is temporarily occupied by Old St. Mary's Chinese School.

▶ Turn left across the street to the mini-park at Himmelman Pl. It is supported by Open Space funds, but its appearance alternates between being maintained and being neglected. Return to Broadway.

▶ At the corner of Broadway and Taylor, there is a high retaining wall with decorative edging along the top. Grading of the slopes in the 1860s and 1870s created vertical bluffs. When the streets were lowered, retaining walls and stairways became necessary to protect the houses perched on the top. Walk up the sidewalk stairway on the south side of Broadway for a better view of No. 1020, which is located up high and toward the back of the property. This two-story, brown-shingle, Craftsman-style house was designed by Albert Farr in 1909.

▶ Ascend the Florence Stairway next to No. 1032 Broadway and notice the concrete wall topped with spindle decoration, and the brass plaque that states ATKINSON-NICHOLS LANDMARK BULDING—1858. There's something strange about this stairway: as you approach each landing, the landscape also seems to rise. Nos. 37 and 39 Florence are Pueblo Revival-style with stucco exteriors and deep-set window apertures to deflect the sun. Robert A. Stern has redesigned No. 40, the original Livermore house on Vallejo.

▶ When you reach Vallejo (Gelett Burgess lived at the corner in the 1890s), cross the street into Russian Hill Place. Nos. 1, 3, 5, and 7 Russian Hill Place are Willis Polk houses of 1913, built for Norman Livermore. It's hard to believe that Russian Hill possesses such a concentration of bewitching little streets in such a small area!

◤ Return to Vallejo and turn right to walk down the ramp to Jones; turn right to Green, and make a left turn. Walk on the south side, the odd-numbered side. The 1000 block of Green was spared from the earthquake and fire of 1906, so it's architecturally notable. No. 1011, a brown-shingled house built after the earthquake, was designed around windows previously in the family's possession. No. 1039–43 is an Italianate of the 1880s and was moved here after 1906. No. 1040 was once the home of the Folger family, whose fortune was made from importing, roasting, and packaging coffee. No. 1055 Green dates from 1866 and was later remodeled by Julia Morgan. The beautiful carriage house at the rear is now used as living quarters. You can also see the 1857 octagon house, the oldest in the City, at No. 1067 Green. A cupola was added in the 1880s. Octagon houses were in vogue for a while because they were purported to be beneficial to your health and sexual vigor. (If you wish to tour the interior of an octagon house, check the hours of the Colonial Dames Octagon at 2645 Gough; call 441-7512.) Engine Company No. 31 formerly occupied the 1907 Tudor Revival-style firehouse across the street. It is now a National Trust Property.

◤ When you reach Hyde, turn right, and then left on Union St. This is the center of the neighborhood shopping area. A restaurant now stands where the Marcel and Henri charcuterie served the community for 20 years. Various members of the same family ran the Home Drug at 1200 Union from 1911–1994. The second pharmacist-owner closed it in 2000 because he could neither compete with chain drugstores nor comply with MediCare regulations. The Searchlight Market has been here for one hundred years under various owners. The original Swensen's ice cream parlor, here since 1948, still makes ice cream on the premises. Le Valet Cleaners has been here since 1951. These shopkeepers provide continuity and stability that contribute to the intangible that is Russian Hill.

◤ Continue west on Union to Polk, turn right to Filbert and your beginning.

San Francisco

Architectural

Signatures

From the vantage point of Pacific Heights, Russian Hill appears to be shaped like a shoe with a square toe. Coincidentally, many sections of Russian Hill are accessible only to walkers. The redwood-shingled, Craftsman-style homes, designed by Northern California architects Julia Morgan, Willis Polk, and Bernard Maybeck in the early 1900s, blend well into this terrain. Irregularly-shaped, deep lots abound; some houses—the kind I call "tuck-ins"—are almost invisible from the street. These tuck-ins are as much a part of the City's architectural signature as the loftier towers you see on this walk.

▶ The beginning point is the northeast corner of Polk St. and Greenwich, where Russian Hill begins its sharp rise toward Larkin Street. Walk north on Polk and pass the four-story Greenwich Court condominium that takes up three fourths of the block. Built of cinder block and redwood, this 1989 structure is painted a pleasing mid-gray color with white window trim, giving the street added lightness. The apartment house next to it is an elaborate Spanish-style building in white stucco.

*In 1821 at the age of 60, Adam Link walked from his home in
Pennsylvania to Ohio (141 miles in 3 days).*

- Turn right on Lombard to see the No. 1299 address of the apartment
  house, the ceramic-tiled step risers, decorative metal on the doors,
  and bas-relief on the pillars. The 1200 block of Lombard beautifully
  illustrates the congeniality between the interspersed Italianates and
  Craftsman-style homes, and between the homes and their hillside
  location. Nos. 1275 and 1259 are large Italianates; 1267–1263 are
  redwood-shingled refurbished Victorians of 1877. The earliest record
  of water hookup for No. 1257 is May 1878. No. 1249, a San
  Francisco Stick Italianate, is a beautiful flat-front tuck-in with a staircase. Built on a hill, it is doubly imposing with its tall false front.

- Cross Lombard at No. 1249 to walk down the Culebra Terrace
  Stairway. The hard-to-see sign is on the side of No. 1246. This is a
  stairway with 29 steps, three landings, and a coda of two steps.

- Culebra is a charming alley of flats and single dwellings enhanced by
  trees, shrubbery, and flowers. No. 60 has a terrazzo stairway and

decorative small tiles; No. 50 has an eye-catching, curved, five-windowed second story. Nos. 35 and 25 are simple cottages. No. 23 was built in 1911.

▲ You emerge from Culebra onto the Chestnut St. cul-de-sac. On our right at the corner is No. 1141, a four-storied series of angled sections to maximize sun and views for the residents. Walk up the wide Chestnut Stairway shadowed by Monterey pines, with gardens on either side.

▲ Forty-eight steps bring you to a landing where a U-shaped double stairway begins. Walk up the right-hand one to Larkin Street. Looking back down the Greenwich corridor, you can see the northwest side of San Francisco; from the top of the stairs note the two dominant landmarks of that part of the City—the unmistakable dome of the Palace of Fine Arts (Walk 8), and the towers of the Golden Gate Bridge.

▲ Turn right on Larkin. A house on the corner has a brass plaque: 2677 LARKIN AT CHESTNUT. (I wish the architect's name and the date were also cited.)

▲ Continue one block to Lombard St. At the southeast corner walk up the stairway into George Sterling Park, named for the poet who lived on Russian Hill during the 1920s. He is remembered for his descrip-

WALK 5: Russian Hill North Route

Public Transportation: Muni Bus #19 runs on Polk; #42, #47, #49 run on Van Ness (walk one block east to Polk).

1. Begin at Polk and Greenwich.
2. Walk north on Polk.
3. Right on Lombard. Cross Lombard at No. 1249.
4. Descend Culebra Terrace Stwy.
5. Right up Chestnut Stwy. to Larkin.
6. Right on Larkin. Continue on Larkin to Lombard.
7. Ascend Stwy. to George Sterling Park. Bear left on path to Greenwich Stwy.
8. Walk on Stwy. to Hyde.
9. Left on Hyde to Lombard to Chestnut.
10. Detour to 1000 block Chestnut. Return to Hyde and go left.
11. Right on Francisco. Bear right to Chestnut.
12. Across from No. 960 walk up Stwy. to Montclair to Lombard.
13. Detour right to No. 2319 Hyde. Return to Lombard to Larkin.
14. Left on Larkin to Greenwich.
15. Right on Greenwich to Polk and your beginning.

tion of San Francisco as the "cool gray city of love." The low-lying trunks of leptospermum trees and the nodules of exposed roots along the path give you a feeling of entering ancient woods. A bench has been thoughtfully placed to permit a meditative view northwest to the Marin hills.

▶ Bear left on the path past the bench (to the sound of tennis balls against racquets above us). Ascend the Greenwich Stairway; pass the upper landing on Phoebe's Terrace (named for a neighborhood bene-factor), past benches and a mosaic tile wall onto the sidewalk. Tennis and basketball players gradually come into view on the left.

▶ The Alice Marble Tennis Courts, also part of the 2.6-acre park, are on Water Department land, the Lombard reservoir beneath supply-ing six to eight surrounding blocks. Alice Marble (1913–1990) was born in the small California town of Dutch Flat, and spent some of her adolescent years in San Francisco. She joined the Golden Gate Park Tennis Club, a training ground for many outstanding players and, during 1936–1940, was a four-time winner of the National Women's Singles Tennis championship.

▶ Descend 26 steps to Hyde, turn left facing Alcatraz (another San Francisco signature), and continue to Lombard. No. 2222 is a steel-framed, reinforced-concrete, white, eight-story cooperative (1920), one of five built by T. Paterson Ross in the Russian Hill neighbor-hood. His buildings are rich in interior detail and utilize the latest technology of that era. Ross designed about 200 buildings during a 32-year period. When he sustained brain injuries from falling bricks in an open freight elevator while inspecting the Union League Club, his professional career ended. He was 49 then but lived until age 84.

▶ The intersection of Hyde and Lombard is a splendid place to stop and see the Hyde Street cable car lurching along with its standing-room-only crowd of passengers. Accorded the conductor's full approval, they alight en masse with their cameras pointed toward Alcatraz, the Bay Bridge, or Treasure Island. At the clang of the cable car bell, they rush aboard once more to coast down to the next land-ing on their way to Aquatic Park.

▶ Continue walking north on Hyde to Chestnut. An inappropriately-placed high-rise on the corner still suffers that friendless look. On the northeast corner of Chestnut and Hyde was a landmark 12-room house built in 1852 by William Clark, who built the first wharf near the foot of Broadway (Walk 1).

Chestnut Street

- Detour left on Chestnut to experience the ambiance of the 1000 block. Between Nos. 1000 and 1080 is a delightful series of three-story, mansard-roofed homes painted white and off-white. The south side of the street features the back entrance of the award-winning Lombardia complex (10 large town houses and 32 condos), designed by architects Hood/Miller, on a lot that was vacant for 28 years. By thoughtful use of scale, space, light, and plant materials, they created an inviting Mediterranean setting. No. 1089 Chestnut, completed in 1990, has 17-foot ceilings in the living room and 5600 square feet of space.

- Return to Hyde, turn left (north), and walk on the right side of the street past the Norwegian Seaman's Church at No. 2454 Hyde. (The Norwegian Government Seamen's Service at 2501 Vallejo is another indication of the number of Norwegian sailors who make port here.) No. 2434 is a five-sided bay Italianate. From the left side of Hyde you can see the roof of another reservoir. Straight ahead (north) is the Hyde Street Pier with its famous collection of historic ships. At the end of the block, descend three steps and turn right onto Francisco St.

- The Francisco cul-de-sac is one of my favorites. The large homes here, designed in a variety of architectural styles, are set on several levels of land to command enviable views from either side of the street.

- The frame two-story at No. 825 is originally dated 1849 but has undergone many renovations. It was constructed of timber salvaged from ships abandoned in the Bay during the Gold Rush. No. 828 Francisco, at the end of the cul-de-sac, has a bay of leaded windows with octagonal inserts, a modified mansard roof, and beautiful copper chimney stacks, which have acquired a greenish cast over the years. A fence espaliered with roses follows the slope of the hill.

- From the parapet next to No. 800 Francisco, you can gaze at the variety of geometric shapes and signatures that are part of a San Franciscan's daily eyeful: the abundant, sword-shaped leaves of a palm tree at the lower corner of the street, the square Romanesque tower of the San Francisco Art Institute, the rectangular towers of the Bay Bridge, the conical towers of Saints Peter and Paul Church in North Beach, the cylindrical Coit Tower, and the pyramidal Transamerica building.

- Walk along the retaining wall, bearing right (south) to Chestnut.

- Turn right on Chestnut. No. 930 has a flat roof, while No. 944, built in 1864, has columns and a balcony. Across the street from No. 960 ascend 28 steps to Montclair Terrace, a hidden court of homes and gardens. No. 66, designed in 1956 by one of my favorite architects, Henry Hill, has simplicity and flourish. Next to No. 4 you're at Lombard St., where drivers enjoy the unusual ride down the most photographed, photogenic hairpin-turn street in the country: eight turns within an 800-foot-long section with a grade of 18.18%. City engineer Preston Wallace King designed it in 1922, from a 26% grade, cobble-stoned Lombard.

- Turn right to walk up a straight, comfortable stairway. At the top, detour right on Hyde to see No. 2319, a Willis Polk house designed for Robert Louis Stevenson's widow, Fanny, who lived there from 1899 to 1908. (Lombard and Hyde was purported to be Stevenson's favorite San Francisco corner.) Return to Lombard and walk right to Larkin; turn left. Among the apartment houses is a two-flat Victorian, No. 2545–2543. No. 2531 is a Stick-style Italianate with a picket fence. No. 2515 has rectangular bays and a fish-scale pediment above the windows.

- Turn right on Greenwich to walk down a grooved sidewalk. No. 1342–1344 is a new condominium in pleasing pastel colors. The garage has been embellished with a band of decorative ceramic tile placed above its doors. Your high spirits will continue as you stride by No. 1356, an interesting angular design of concrete landings and steps surrounded by large, leafy trees, to arrive at your beginning.

A Segmented

FORT MASON

Walk

On this walk you explore some of the extensive municipal and federal recreational areas of San Francisco along the northern waterfront. Walking west from the Marina Green through Presidio lands or east from the Marina Green to the Hyde St. Pier, you can appreciate how this land became a focus for federal military installations, and then slowly evolved, under the aegis of the Department of the Interior, into land for a national park. The area you traverse is part of the Golden Gate National Recreation Area (GGNRA), the most popular urban park in the United States. More apparent here than in other neighborhoods is how the continuum of past history blends into an evolving contemporary scene. Naturally, the atmosphere is highly energized.

The most propitious time to go on the Fort Mason walk is in the morning—a sunny, windless morning. While this extensive walk fits together organically, its shape also suggests you can easily divide it into two—Segment 1 and Segment 2.

To maximize your options at the end of the walk, I suggest coming to the beginning point by public transportation. However, if you arrive by car, drive into the parking section near Scott and Marina for Segment 1. Drive into the Ft. Mason parking lot facing Marina Blvd., across the street from Safeway, for Segment 2.

Segment 1

▶ From the Marina Green at Scott and Marina, follow the path to the water and turn left onto the Coastal Trail to reach the newly restored Crissy Field, a 20-acre tidal marsh, a new shoreline promenade, and a restored beach and dunes. A community environmental center will be built in 2001. (Prior to 1915, Crissy Field was used as a dump by the Army; in the 1920s the space was used for an airfield and a rifle range.) You can continue on the trail to Fort Point (built in 1861 for defense against the South during the Civil War). Its walls are seven feet thick and 45 feet high, and it survived the 1906 earthquake.

▶ Retrace your steps to the beginning of the Crissy Field trail section, then turn left (east) toward the San Francisco Yacht Club to reach the Wave Organ at the jetty's end. This wave-activated acoustic sculpture was designed by Peter Richards, and built by sculptor and master stonemason, George Gonzalez, under the aegis of the Exploratorium. It is situated in the sound garden the artists designed, a terraced amphitheater built of recycled marble and granite acquired from a dismantled cemetery. The idea was to sit, enjoy the view of the skyline, and listen to the water music as the pipes—which extend down into the Bay—respond to the movement of the water. The project was completed in spring of 1986 as part of the Exploratorium's science/art collection, and was dedicated to Frank Oppenheimer, founding director. Unfortunately, after a few years the Organ filled with silt, and the music is only heard through some of the pipes. But the views and the unusual garden setting are still enlivening. Return.

Edward Payson Weston began a 500-mile walk on May 25, 1908 from San Francisco to Los Angeles. People were invited to join him at any point and walk as far as they wanted. He left the Olympic Club on Post St. at 12:00 noon, sharp. He reached Los Angeles in 10 days.

Scott St. and Marina Blvd. was the site of the 1915 Panama-Pacific International Exposition. This extravagant and most classic of fairs signaled all the world that San Francisco, like the mythical Phoenix, had arisen from the ashes of the 1906 earthquake to become again the City that everybody loves.

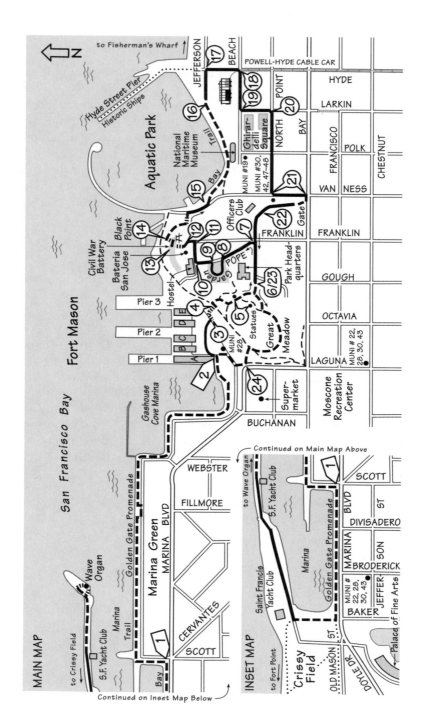

WALK 6: Fort Mason Route

Public Transportation: For Segment 1: Muni Bus #30 along Stockton to Broderick and Jefferson; walk one block north to Marina Blvd. and one block west (left) to Baker. For Segment 2: Bus #28 runs on Chestnut St. and into the Ft. Mason parking lot.

Segment 1

1. Begin at Scott and Marina. Follow path along the water; turn left onto path of Coastal Trail that will take you through Crissy Field to Fort Point. Retrace steps to beginning of Crissy Field trail section, then continue left, toward the S.F. Yacht Club and the jetty's end. Return from jetty. *(Optional) If you want to continue into Ft. Mason (and Segment 2), walk along the water, curving around E. Harbor Breakwater. Continue on Gashouse Cove Marina path.*

Segment 2

2. Begin at the side of Bldg. A in Lower Fort Mason.
3. Walk up the Stwy. opposite Bldg. E.
4. Walk on any of the paths around or through the Great Meadow.
5. Pass Bufano sculpture, *Peace.* Pass Phillip Burton Memorial.
6. Left on MacArthur to Park Headquarters (Bldg. No. 201).
7. Left on Pope.
8. Walk around Community Gardens and out on Pope.
9. Left on Pope.
10. Right on Funston.
11. Left on Franklin.
12. Curve to left on Stwy. to Bateria San Jose.
13. Descend Stwy. to Battery. Walk on sidewalk to picnic area; descend Stwy. to Black Point.
14. Right on footpath; descend Stwy. to Promenade.
15. Right along Promenade.
16. Continue on Jefferson to Hyde.
17. Right on Hyde to Beach.
18. Right on Beach to Larkin. (Be sure to first walk through Ghirardelli Square.)
19. Left on Larkin to North Point.
20. Right on North Point to Van Ness. Check bus schedules for #30, #42, and #47–49.
21. Left on Van Ness to Bay. Turn right immediately into the first gate of Ft. Mason.
22. Pass Ft. Mason Officers' Club.
23. Left at McDowell Hall, past sculpture, bearing left toward public bathrooms.
24. At bottom of hill, across from Safeway, you are near your beginning.

Ironically, the underlying foundation of the Marina's existence—water—together with the unstable fill and the construction of non-earthquake-code buildings, caused catastrophic damage to the neighborhood during the November 17, 1989 earthquake (7.1 on the Richter scale). Residents left the area to find housing in other parts of the City, and some Chestnut St. businesses closed permanently. (Other neighborhoods where streams or lakes once had existed also sustained damage.)

▲ Follow the Promenade along the water, in the direction of Fillmore St. (east), curving around the East Harbor Breakwater. In the water alongside you see coots, western grebes, and mallards. Mallow, oxalis, and tower of jewels bloom beside the walkway.

Segment 2 (begins alongside Bldg. A in lower Ft. Mason)

▲ Continue on the Gashouse Cove Marina path and enter Fort Mason by the side of Bldg. A. (Pick up a calendar of events at the Fort Mason Foundation office, or call (415) 441-3400.) For many years this was the point of embarkation for men and supplies. The Army used the buildings alongside the piers through demobilization after World War II and the Korean conflict. They are now used for recreational and cultural activities. Lower Fort Mason, which is managed and administered by the nonprofit Fort Mason Foundation, is the headquarters for more than 50 nonprofit community and cultural organizations. These include theaters, museums, music schools, dance classes, computer groups, the Children's Art Center, and Lawyers for the Arts. Greens Restaurant in Bldg. A is an excellent vegetarian restaurant operated by the Tassajara Zen Center.

▲ In Fort Mason (named for the first military governor of California), an area of about 89 acres, you can trace a continuous evolving historical line from 1797 to the present, from Spanish and American military fortifications to a section of the Golden Gate National Recreation Area. The integration of history and land-use objectives is resulting in a unification of the past and present. For instance, as military artifacts from the past are unearthed, they are placed for viewing in contextual areas, necessitating the redesign of spaces and trails. More recent history is also being commemorated: the Phillip Burton Memorial was re-landscaped to accommodate better viewing of the sculpture, the green spaces and new paths.

- You pass Bldgs. A, B, C, D, and E, and Piers 1 and 2 and the Festival Pavilion. The J. Porter Shaw Library in Bldg. E has an extensive collection of maritime history books, periodicals, and oral histories of the West Coast. It is open to the general public.

- As you continue walking along the wall, note the stern of *The Galilee*, a Tahitian trading vessel, which was built in 1891 and was in use until 1920. The Oceanic Society has its offices nearby.

- Opposite Bldg. E is a stairway. As I walked up the first series of steps, I saw hummingbirds dipping and revolving around one another in their courtship ritual. A Monterey cypress is on the left.

- The next level at Fort Mason features former military housing, the International Hostel, and the GGNRA headquarters—a resource for information about the entire national park system as well as community conservation issues, (415) 556-0560. The Park Service continually monitors problem areas. They plant soil-huggers like sand verbena, ice-plant, and dune daisy to restrain the constantly shifting, sandy soil. They build stairways to prevent erosion, preserve the fragile topsoil, and keep people on the trails. Turn around to see the Marina Blvd., the Golden Gate Bridge, and the Marin Headlands. Take the path to the left, walking counterclockwise toward the Great Meadow. You are retracing the long-forgotten footsteps of hundreds of men, women, and children who lived here in tents after losing their homes in the 1906 earthquake. Refugee Camp No. 5 extended west beyond the meadow to the site of the present Safeway store.

- Fort Mason was an important site during and after the 1906 earthquake. The Navy fireboat anchored here was used to pump water from the Bay to the fire engines along Van Ness. Fort Mason was the headquarters for General Funston, who had to put San Francisco under martial law to prevent looting. Subsequently, under General Greely, it became the relief-supply distribution center. When Mayor Schmitz moved his office here, Fort Mason became the center for coordinating civil and military authority.

- Following the paved footpath to the right, you reach the Beniamino Bufano sculpture of cast stone and mosaic dedicated to *Peace*. Bufano (1898–1970) was a favorite San Francisco personality. He was supported by various benefactors, such as the owner of the Powell St. restaurant (now defunct) for which he designed and executed a mosaic mural in return for a lifetime of meals.

▲ Walk along the path to the Phillip Burton Memorial, designed by landscape architect Tito Patri; the project sculptor was Wendy Ross. The 10-foot sculpture of Burton represents him in his everyday look—rumpled trousers, emphatic gesture, a scribbled note in his jacket pocket. In 1983, Congress dedicated the GGNRA to Congressman Burton, who was responsible for the Federal legislation that made the Park a reality. The sculpture was unveiled in spring 1991. (If you look to the right, you can see the Palace of Fine Arts dome.)

▲ Continue east on the path to Park Headquarters, Bldg. No. 201 on MacArthur Street. It was built in 1901 as a military hospital. After the 1906 earthquake, it was used as an emergency center and a lying-in hospital. According to legend, eight babies were born at Fort Mason the night after the quake.

▲ In the years following 1906, Bldg. No. 201 was used as administrative headquarters for Fort Mason. During World War II Ronald Reagan (President of the United States, 1981–1989) served here as second lieutenant in charge of tracking down missing shipments. Fort Mason was declared a National Historic Landmark in 1985.

▲ Make a left turn on Pope Rd. to pass around headquarters. To your right, near the corner of Franklin, are the Mission Revival-style Chapel (1942) and the starting place of the Conversation-Pace Game field, sponsored by the San Francisco Senior Center. Various exercises here are paced slowly enough to allow for conversation.

▲ Turn left on Shafter into the Community Garden to explore greenhouses, latticeworks, and terraces, and view the enormous variety of plants and vegetables and flowers in cultivation. Several gardeners specialize in rare varieties of flowers. The Ft. Mason garden is very popular and, even though space is available to anyone who applies, the average wait time is four years. Return to Pope, and go left.

▲ The San Francisco International Hostel at the end of Pope, Bldg. 240, formerly a Civil War barracks, is a friendly, clean, and inviting place. You may see some of the guests lolling about on the grass, while others may be reading. The hostel can accommodate 70; there is 24-hour access and no curfew.

▲ From the hostel turn right on Funston and left on Franklin. This part of Fort Mason contains military residences dating from the 1850s. The officers' housing on the east side of Pope St. originated as squatters' homes, put up in the 1850s by prominent San Franciscans who understood the value of the real estate. The Army took possession of the homes and began building up fortifications in anticipation of a Confederate attack.

▶ Strong pro- and anti-slavery feelings in California culminated in the famous Terry-Broderick duel in 1859. Senator David Broderick, shot by the hot-tempered pro-slavery Judge David Terry near Lake Merced, died here at Fort Mason in the home of a friend.

▶ Continue north on Franklin along the concrete walkway. You pass the Palmer House erected in 1855. Then you reach an open green space on the left, where John Fremont's home was from 1859–1861. Go up the stairs to the left to see the plaque (rusty) noting the site of the Bateria San Jose, a Spanish seacoast defense battery located here in 1797. It was built to protect the Yerba Buena anchorage, now Aquatic Park. Continue to the first light standard, passing the intertwined Monterey cypress and laurel trees. Pass light standard No. 43, and then turn right down the short stairway. Walk across the area of the battery emplacements in the wall. At the western end the sign reads 1863 BATTERY, next to the railroad-tie steps that you climb. But first, glance left to take in the depths of the open battery.

▶ When you reach the top of the stairs, look down on the piers. Continue to the right along a concrete sidewalk toward the picnic section. You are standing on what is known as Black Point Lookout, so called because of the dark vegetation provided by the laurel trees. The picnic area was constructed on battery platforms that date to the Civil War. There are four tables and benches where you can sit to enjoy food and the sublime view, which, when I visited, featured a procession of boats with multicolored sails of pink and green and blue, backlit against the clearly delineated hills of Marin and the East Bay.

▶ Theoretically, the Bay was well defended against hostile fleets. At one time or another there were Spanish or American coastal batteries on the Marin Headlands, Alcatraz, Angel Island, Fort Point, and here at Fort Mason. The best preserved of these antiquated defenses is Fort Point, the Civil War fort under the arch of the Golden Gate Bridge (Segment 1).

▶ Descend a stairway and follow a long, paved walkway, where benches have conveniently been placed, passing a gate that leads to a private residence. At that point, bear left down the stairs to street level. On the left you can see the small, fenced wood section of what was formerly the Alcatraz Pier. Here, convicts boarded a boat for the

Fort Mason

island prison. In front is Aquatic Pier, the first major public pier in San Francisco (1934). Follow the path to the right.

▶ The curved concrete wall of Aquatic Park, formerly known as Black Point Cove, was once part of the San Jose Point Military Reservation, which became Fort Mason in 1882. Pumping Station No. 2, built to supply water in case of earthquake and fire, is on the right side of the street. Also on the right is the tunnel, bored into the rocks under Fort Mason, through which the Belt Line Railroad tracks ran. The Belt Line, opened in 1896, covered the City front from Islais Creek to the Presidio. The original purpose was to move boxcars and flat-cars directly alongside cargo vessels. In the late 1920s they carried men and military supplies to the Presidio; in the late 1950s the tracks were filled in by the military.

▶ Cross the extension of Van Ness Ave. to be on the waterside. Public restrooms are housed in the white structure—with incised wavy lines near the roofline to simulate ocean waves—an example of the Streamline Moderne style of the 1930s. (The twin of this one is located at the end of Jefferson St.) Walk on the Promenade along the water and ascend the amphitheater steps to watch birds and swimmers.

▶ The ship-shaped Maritime Museum to the right was founded in 1950 by Karl Kortum. Its holdings include many artifacts of the sea, permanent exhibits of historic ship models that plied the Pacific Coast, and an excellent collection of prints. They arrange special exhibitions, and well-informed rangers are available to answer questions. The very active senior center (the oldest nonprofit one in the United States, 1947) also uses part of the 1939 Moderne building, which was built as a WPA project during the Franklin Roosevelt administration.

▶ Walk east on Jefferson, passing the Dolphin and Swim Club established in 1877. Members still swim in the Bay. Next to it is the South End Rowing Club.

▶ Historic ships are docked at the Hyde St. Pier, and one can take an imaginary trip: on the *Eureka*, a passenger ferry; the *Thayer*, a sailing schooner that carried lumber, salmon, and codfish; or the *Wapama*, a steam schooner for cargo and passengers. A nominal fee to board the ships helps defray the expense of preserving them. The bookstore has an excellent collection pertaining to the sea and related subjects. At the corner of Hyde, on the right-hand side, is a pumping station that dates from 1948.

- Turn right on Hyde St. and walk along the side of Victoria Park (designed by Thomas Church in 1960), which is festive with a gazebo and flowers, and the Cable Car turntable. Jovial crowds of tourists and residents wait to board. Turn right on Beach.

- Musicians and performers are interspersed among the outdoor stall displays of jewelry, T-shirts, leather belts, pen and ink drawings of San Francisco scenes, and stained-glass mobiles and window insets.

- Continue to Larkin. Ghirardelli Square, at the corner, is a pioneer example of adaptive use of the former chocolate factory (1893). It was converted in 1967 into a well-designed complex of fine-quality specialty shops, galleries, and restaurants. The entrance, via stairways to the plaza, is particularly pleasing. Walk up the stairway to the plaza, where people sit around a fountain designed by Ruth Asawa. The open spaces, the many areas set aside for meals al fresco, the nearness to the street, and the Bay views from many sections create a seductive environment for browsing or buying, or for an enjoyable day in the City that feels like a vacation.

- Walk out from the plaza in any direction to reach North Point. Go right (west) to Van Ness and turn left to Bay, immediately turning right into the first gate of Fort Mason. Building No. 9 is used for children's social services. Pass the Fort Mason Officers' Club, which is open to the public for dinner and available for rental. Go left at McDowell Hall, past the sculpture, bearing left toward the public bathrooms and the new plantings. At the bottom of the hill you are across from the Safeway and near your beginning.

Walk Forward

PACIFIC HEIGHTS

but Always Look Back

When the first cable car went over Nob Hill in 1878, the development of Pacific Heights, the ridge across the Polk-Van Ness Valley, soon followed. Then as now, the views of the Bay were extraordinary. Although a precipitous 370 feet above sea level, the Heights had many wide, flat lots for the large homes only the wealthy could afford.

The variety of architectural styles range from Italianates of the late 1870s, elaborate Queen Anne Victorians of the 1890s, Mission Revival, Edwardian, Italian Renaissance, to mock Chateau. Pacific Heights is an excellent area to practice sightings of architectural details—general, singular, and humorous.

▶ Begin at Broadway and Baker St. Bliss and Faville, famous for their designs of classical government buildings built No. 2898 Broadway, on the northeast corner, in 1889. (A few blocks away on Broadway, toward the end of this walk, you will see another Bliss and Faville structure to compare.)

▶ Walk north down the two-block-long Baker Stairway. Monterey pines and cypresses in the center area and dense shrubs on both sides confine the stairway. In addition, the tread to riser proportion of the stairs is not felicitous.

▶ Entering Vallejo St. from the stairway, you walk into a cul-de-sac with handsome river stones embedded on the slope. The large home on your left at No. 2901 Vallejo, built in 1886, is a combination of Mediterranean and Mission styles. Turn right to look at No. 2881, which has an extremely narrow second-story window.

▶ Return to Baker to descend the lower section of the stairway, which seems lighter and more cheerful than the upper section. Open space around the comfortable stairs makes this a happy, bouncy descent. No. 2511 is a redwood-shingled box with a twin-gabled roof.

> *There is no orthodoxy in walking. It is a land of many paths*
> *and no paths, where everyone goes his own way and is right.*
> —Dr. Trevelyan

▶ The Palace of Fine Arts is in the center of view, surrounded by the North Bay and the circle of hills beyond it. Twin houses at Nos. 2800 and 2828 Green that I find particularly appealing are to our left. Go to the end of the Green St. cul-de-sac to look at the variety and the unity of the architecture.

▶ Come back to the corner of Baker and continue walking along Green to Fillmore. No. 2790 is the Russian Consulate. No. 2452 is a tuck-in; No. 2423, built in 1891, has a ramp to the house, and the archi-

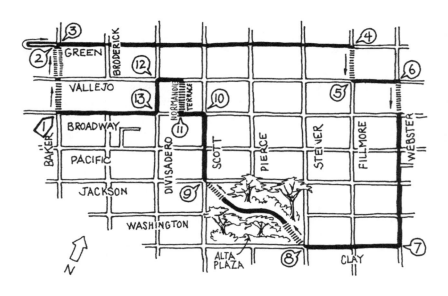

tect, Ernest Coxhead, built his own house next door at No. 2421. No. 2411 has a slate roof. The street between Pierce and Steiner is barricaded during the lunch hour so students from St. Vincent de Paul School can play in the street.

▶ The odd-numbered houses in the 2200 block of Green between Steiner and Fillmore have high retaining walls—a reminder of the original height of the hill. (If you would like to see the Sherman House, an exquisite Bed & Breakfast, walk one block farther to No. 2160 Green. It was built in 1867 for Leander Sherman of Sherman Clay music stores, and designed especially for musical gatherings. Artists such as Madame Schumann-Heink and Ignace Jan Paderewski performed there. In back of the B & B is an elaborate carriage house with a mansard roof that has shingles in alternating patterns of diamonds and octagons. Some of the walk lights in front of the carriage house reveal the purple tint of oxidation.)

▶ Ascend the Fillmore (sidewalk) Stairway from Green to Vallejo. Note the difference in walking comfort between the stairway on the left, an L-shaped tread, and the one on the right, a sloping tread. No. 2323 Vallejo is the Vedanta Society Temple designed by Henry Gutterson and completed in 1959. The architecture is more subdued than the 1905 original temple on Filbert and Webster. Both Temples

WALK 7: Pacific Heights Route

Public Transportation: Muni Bus #3 goes to Jackson and Baker; #45 goes to Union and Baker.

1. Begin at Baker and Broadway. Descend Baker Stwy. to Vallejo, the sidewalk Stwy. down to Green.
2. Left on Green to view cul-de-sac.
3. Head east on Green to Fillmore.
4. Right to ascend Stwy. to Vallejo.
5. Left on Vallejo.
6. Right on Webster Stwy. Continue on Webster to Clay.
7. Right on Clay to Steiner.
8. Walk up the Clay Stwy. of Alta Plaza Park. Walk across in a westerly direction to Jackson and Scott.
9. Right on Scott to Broadway.
10. Left on Broadway for one-half block to Normandie Terrace.
11. Go to end of cul-de-sac. Descend Stwy. to Vallejo. Left on Vallejo to Divisadero.
12. Left on Divisadero to Broadway.
13. Right on Broadway to Baker and your beginning.

are in use. The basic philosophic tenet of Vedantism is that all paths to God are equally true. Everything comes from the divine spirit, and the purpose of life is to discover that unfolding spirit within us and everywhere else. Nearby are the monastery and convent, where men and women train to become monastics.

▶ Turn left on Vallejo for one block. The graceless apartment structure at No. 2295 is a vivid contrast to No. 2255, four charming brick and stucco set-back apartments built on two levels, sharing a common stairway and a landscaped courtyard. At Webster, walk up the stairway to Broadway. At the top is one of San Francisco's most famous views. Nos. 2120 and 2222 Broadway are two estates that belonged to the Flood family (of the Comstock mines) and are now private schools. The former, built in 1898 for James C. Flood, is the Sarah Dix Hamlin School for Girls. The gardens and tennis courts extend the depth of the lot to No. 2129 Vallejo, where an addition to the school was built in 1965; the two buildings are connected by a stairway. No. 2222 Broadway, the Convent of the Sacred Heart High School, was designed in 1912 for James L. Flood, J.C.'s son. This Italian Renaissance-style mansion by Bliss and Faville has an exterior of Tennessee marble; the interior has hand-carved wood paneling of oak, satinwood, and walnut. (I'm sure the Hebrew tradition of placing honey on the first page of the first book a child reads, to promote sweet associations with learning, applies as well to learning in such beautiful surroundings.)

▶ Though it displays the pineapple finial, a symbol for hospitality, No. 2550 Webster is a heavy looking, uninviting, clinker-brick structure. Willis Polk built it in 1896 for William Bourn, who at various times was head of the Spring Valley Water Company, Pacific Gas and Electric, and the Empire Mining Company in Grass Valley. Polk also designed Filoli, Bourn's garden estate in Woodside, now part of the National Trust for Historic Preservation.

▶ The Newcomer High School at Jackson and Webster provides bilingual classes and transitional education for recently arrived immigrant students.

▶ At Nos. 2321–2315 Webster, between Jackson and Washington, are a series of slanted-bay Italianates that date from 1878. Hollyhocks and roses growing in the gardens complement the simple character of the houses. In the next block, between Washington and Clay, is a series of attached, slanted-bay Italianates, Nos. 2253–2233. These homes are in the Webster Historic District. Yet another group of

Italianates, Nos. 2221–2209, round out the picture we glean of the Victorian community. The California Pacific Medical Center, which presently dominates the area, has evolved from a merger of the University of Pacific Medical School and Presbyterian Hospital.

▲ Turn right on Clay. One block ahead on Fillmore was the site of a stagecoach stop, currently the shops and offices at No. 2318.

▲ At Steiner you walk up the Clay Stairway of Alta Plaza Park, which was purchased in 1877. John McLaren, the superintendent of Golden Gate Park for 60 years, designed the 12 acres of excessively steep Alta Plaza in the only way possible—with slopes and terraces. The stairways are magnificent and the views varied. Looking down from the hill on the row of Italianates on Clay (Nos. 2637–2673), you appreciate the presence and the scale of these post-Civil War structures.

▲ Walk across the park in a westerly direction toward Jackson and Scott; continue north on Scott to Broadway. Turn left into Normandie Terrace, a special enclave of a few custom-designed homes. At the end of the cul-de-sac, descend the stairway. Turn left on Vallejo and left on Divisadero. Turn right on Broadway. The view from here is another "special." Continue to Baker and your beginning.

Tripping

PRESIDIO WALL & MARINA

Lightly

The Marina neighborhood is one of the most beautiful in the City. The harbor, the boulevard, the Palace of Fine Arts with its surrounding lagoon and paths, Chestnut St., and proximity to the Presidio, are magnets that bring people from everywhere out to enjoy a day in the City.

The Marina has come full circle. It occupies the landfill site of the spectacular Panama-Pacific International Exposition of 1915, which celebrated the rebirth of San Francisco after the 1906 earthquake. In 1989 the Marina, because it is built on landfill, was devastated in the Loma Prieta earthquake. Two years later much of the Marina had been rebuilt. New structures are built and standing ones now retrofitted to earthquake code. Chestnut St., the Marina's authentic and stable shopping area, is again thriving. (Some storekeepers along the street have been in business for over 35 years.)

The walk begins and ends in the Pacific Heights/Presidio Wall area, looping through lower sections of the Marina. You'll experience a contrast in topography and neighborhood ambiance, besides the comfortable feeling that the two neighborhoods fit together after all. Imagine you're on a vacation stroll.

▲ Begin at the 379-foot elevation of the intersection at Pacific and Lyon Streets. This corner was named Cannon Hill for the symbolic cannon placed on the summit to mark the southeast corner of the Presidio (in the late 1870s). Walk north along the Presidio wall, enjoying a view of the Palace of Fine Arts' Romanesque rotunda, with the Marin hills as a backdrop.

▶ At Broadway descend the imposing Lyon St. Stairway—designed by Louis Upton in 1916—an arrangement of stairs, landings, and garden spaces. The Broadway neighbor to the right of the stairway has taken the initiative to renovate the gardens. The slope is covered with ivy. Surprisingly, it has a beautiful, undulating effect as you walk on the stairs. In spring, the blossoms on the plum trees, and the colors and shapes of the annuals planted alongside the stairs, draw you to them. The 130 steps reach a landing on Vallejo before resuming across the street with another 124.

▶ On the ledge of the next set of stairs is a plaque dedicated to the memory of Ann Fogelberg, who spearheaded the Lyon St. Pride Project—the cleanup and the planting of trees and thousands of Vinca major on the slopes of Lyon Stairway between Vallejo and Green. She recruited neighborhood people, high school students, the Dept. of Public Works Environmental Street Services, San Francisco Beautiful, as well as many others.

▶ The stairway ends in the cul-de-sac of Green. The houses to your left stand on part of the Miranda land grant, given to Corporal A. Miranda of the Presidio. The oval center, Ojo de Agua de Figueroa, planted with redwood and cypress, used to be the watering hole for Presidio horses. In 1994 the Army released the Presidio to the Department of the Interior. It is now part of the GGNRA, the Golden Gate National Recreation Area. Basic landscaping has been a priority. Americorp and many volunteers have been working to restore native plants. By law the Presidio must be self-supporting by 2013. To comply with that mandate, office space is rented to various organizations; George Lukas' film company plans to build a campus for the digital/visual arts.

London itself perpetually attracts, stimulates, gives me a play and a story and a poem without any trouble, save that of moving my legs through the streets.

—Virginia Woolf

▶ At Lombard you pass Liverpool Lil's, a well-known pub/restaurant (with great hamburgers) that has been located here since 1973.

▶ Continue north on Lyon (looking back occasionally to view the homes on the heights). Turn right on Francisco to Richardson. Cross Richardson *at the crosswalk* and follow it back to Lyon, which curves slightly to the Palace of Fine Arts. The area around the lagoon is a popular place for people to picnic, sunbathe, and have their wedding parties photographed.

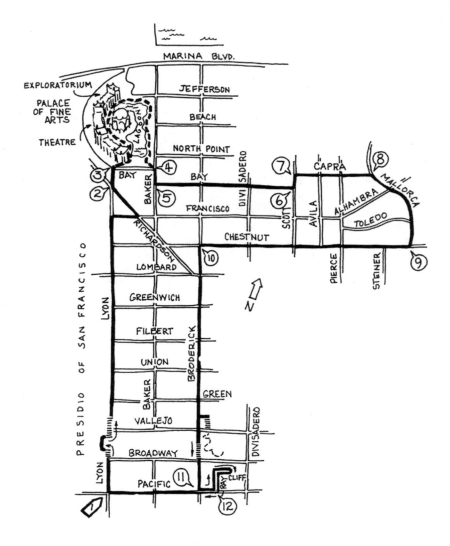

Bear left around the theater to the Exploratorium, a museum where adults and children participate—touching, looking, listening, moving—in experiments that illustrate the scientific principles of perception. The Exploratorium was the idea of the late physicist Dr. Frank Oppenheimer and his wife Jackie. High-school students serve as docents, explaining exhibits. The Exploratorium is one of the most vital museums in the City, and has been a model for science museums throughout the world.

At the Exploratorium's Baker St. exit you turn onto the path that fronts some Baker St. homes and circles the lagoon among the Monterey cypresses. When I was there, I identified a European widgeon, a bufflehead, and some coots. The area on the south side of the lagoon is known as Walter S. Johnson Park. A plaque on a fluted planter states that Johnson contributed generously to preserve the Bernard Maybeck designed Palace of Fine Arts, the only architectural survivor of the 1915 Fair's many temporary structures.

Modified Spanish-style architecture and modified row, bay-windowed bungalows in pastel colors, light gray and light terracotta, typical of the Marina, seem to reflect all the sunlight. Turn left (east) on Bay. A mural of an English touring car is painted on the garage next to No. 2380. A tile inset of a Spanish lady with a mantilla is on

WALK 8: Presidio Wall & Marina Route

Public Transportation: Muni Bus #3 (Jackson) or #43 (Masonic) each stop a block away from your beginning.

1. Begin at Lyon and Pacific. Walk north on Lyon. Turn right on Francisco to Richardson.
2. Cross Richardson, heading along it back to Lyon and toward the Exploratorium.
3. Bear left to walk on Palace Dr. around the back of theater and Exploratorium. Continue around inner courtyard of rotunda and walk among the ruins. At Baker St. entrance of Exploratorium, right on path that circles lagoon.
4. Walk south on Baker to Bay.
5. Left on Bay to Scott.
6. Left on Scott to Capra.
7. Right on Capra to Mallorca.
8. Right on Mallorca to Chestnut.
9. Right on Chestnut to Broderick.
10. Left on Broderick to Pacific.
11. Left on Pacific to Raycliff.
12. Return to Pacific. Right to Lyon and your beginning.

the wall of No. 2375. There are flats and single dwellings along the block. No. 2300 is a 15-unit apartment building. The 1989 earthquake damaged the original building, and the present structure is new. The owner carried earthquake insurance! Many former residents of the Marina have returned because they enjoyed living here and believe that disaster will not strike twice.

► Turn left on Scott and then right on Capra. At the corner of Avila is a beautiful row of two-story dwellings. No. 144–146 is a Spanish-style home with wooden shutters. No. 196 Avila is a two-story tunnel bungalow with a beautiful garden and abundant greenery along the sidewalk. Two apartment buildings at the corner of Pierce were damaged by the 1989 quake.

► Turn right on Mallorca. Note the twin ficus trees at No. 238. If you walk on the right side of Mallorca, you can see the Fillmore hill beyond Chestnut.

► Continue to Chestnut and turn right on the Marina's shopping street. While there is enough foot traffic to create an inviting ambiance, there's still room for strolling and window-shopping. (The stores carry good quality merchandise.) More young people have moved into the neighborhood since the 1989 earthquake, and the stores reflect this demographic change: more coffee houses, more outdoor seating for restaurants, and more beauty supply stores.

► In addition, old favorites are still here. Lucca Delicatessen at No. 2120 has been here since 1929. Their homemade pastas and sauces, barbecued chicken, and custom-made sandwiches attract long lines of customers who visit with one another while waiting. Fireside Camera has been on the street since 1954.

► Peets, at No. 2156, retains the name of Alfred Peet, the person responsible for educating the Bay Area about fine coffees and teas, although he no longer owns it. Fortunately, two experienced coffee people bought it and continue the tradition of Peet's roasting.

► No. 2323 has been a grocery store for approximately 70 years, and Marina Super since 1985. They have charge accounts, take phone orders, and make home deliveries. Bechelli's Coffee Shop at No. 2346 is the oldest restaurant on Chestnut. They serve excellent breakfasts. Mathray's Flowers at No. 2395 and Frank's Shoe Repair at No. 2412 have been on the street since the 1950s. (Frank's has a shoe deposit box in the door.) The apartments at No. 2442 and No. 2465 date from 1930 and 1928.

Lyon Street

▶ Turn left on Broderick to walk uphill. The houses are eclectic and architecturally sound. No. 2821 and the house to the right were the earliest on the block, dating from about 1907.

▶ At Broderick and Vallejo you reach an overpass stairway that leads into the driveway and garage of No. 2798 Broderick. The landscaping here counteracts the steepness of the hill beautifully: three pine trees planted among large riverbed rocks laid out in a pleasing pattern in the center of the street, with cobblestones outlining the margins. Toward Broadway, Broderick becomes a miniature "curly Lombard Street."

▶ First ascend a short stairway and a (sidewalk) stairway to arrive at No. 2800 Broadway, a 1907 Jacobean-style mansion designed by Willis Polk. It features early Renaissance stone archways and leaded windows; the magnolia tree may be blooming out front. No. 2801 Broadway with its Corinthian columns cries out for cascading greenery to clothe the bare walls. From this height, the Palace of Fine Arts seems far away.

▶ Continue on Broderick. At Pacific you detour left about 50 feet into Raycliff Terrace, a cul-de-sac of six houses designed by contemporary architects. Now walk west on Pacific. The El Drisco Hotel at 2901 Pacific (50 rooms) was built as a boardinghouse in 1903; it became a hotel in the 1930s. No. 2950 is a "tuck-in" house, inset some distance from the sidewalk. An unusual variance gives three houses at No. 3070 one driveway with entrances on both Pacific and Lyon St.

▶ At Lyon St. you have reached your beginning.

Sutro's Legacy

for All Time,

Our Responsibility

to the End of Time

You can begin the Lands End walk from either
Point Lobos Ave. on the western end (*Part One*),
or from El Camino Del Mar on the eastern end
(*Part Two*). You can explore side trails from either
direction, and can easily extend the length beyond the
book's coverage.

Part One

Beginning the walk from Point Lobos Ave. puts you immediately in
an area of the City that Adolph Sutro loved for its beauty and ocean air,
and developed for its natural recreation potential. He built the Sutro
Railroad to provide low cost transportation for family outings—swimming in the Sutro Baths, dining at the Cliff House, or walking on the
grounds of his 21-acre Sutro Heights Estate of sculpture and landscaped
gardens.

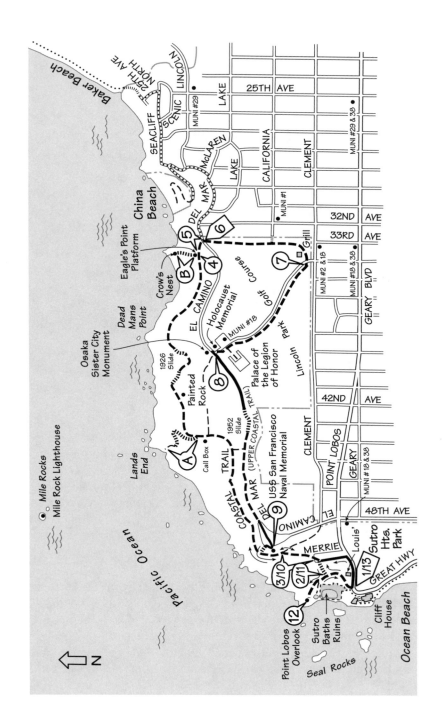

WALK 9: Lands End Route

Part One: *(Walk east on the lower Coastal Trail; return west on the upper Coastal Trail.)*

Public Transportation: Muni Bus #18 stops at Louis' Restaurant and Palace of Legion of Honor. Bus #38 stops at 48th Ave. and Pt. Lobos Ave; walk 2 blocks west.

1. Begin behind Louis' Restaurant at No. 902 Pt. Lobos Ave. and walk down the incline. Follow trail curving to wood Stwy.
2. Ascend the Stwy. to Merrie Way parking lot.
3. Left turn through parking lot to Coastal Trail.
3A. *(optional) Near the LEASH DOG sign, you could descend Lands End Stwy. Use caution. Though it's a regulation trail, the climb back up to the Coastal Trail is difficult. (Lands End is also a nude beach.)*
4. Just before you reach El Camino Del Mar and the Seacliff neighborhood, ascend the stairway on your left to Eagle's Point Platform.
4B. *(optional) Descend the stairway opposite the Platform to Crow's Nest (or as far as you want) for the view; then ascend.*
5. Left on Coastal Trail to El Camino Del Mar and Seacliff; explore this neighborhood if you want.
6. *To return to your beginning via upper Coastal Trail:* Take the dirt trail left (opposite Eagle's Pt.), which skirts the golf course.
7. Bear right along Legion of Honor Dr. Continue right, past the Museum entrance to the Holocaust Memorial, then left past the Osaka Sister City Monument.
8. Continue west along paved road (becoming a trail after a stairway). Where path ends at a parking lot, walk to USS San Francisco Naval Memorial.
9. To the right of the Memorial, descend the stairway to the lower Coastal Trail. Turn left into Merrie Way parking lot.
10. Descend stairway to the Ruins area. Curve right to ascend Pt. Lobos Overlook.
11. Walk left to ascend to Pt. Lobos Ave. and your beginning.

Part Two: *(Beginning from map marker #6, walk west on the upper Coastal Trail; return east on the lower Coastal Trail.)*

Public Transportation: Muni Bus #1 stops at 32nd and Clement; walk two blocks north on 32nd and one block west on El Camino Del Mar to the beginning.

6. Enter the Lands End Trail a few feet from where the trail branches to Eagle's Point Platform; instead, take the dirt trail left around the Lincoln Park Golf Course.
   (Follow directions for markers 7–11 from Part One, and then continue as described below.)
12. Left on Pt. Lobos Ave. to Merrie Way parking lot. Walk through the lot to the start of lower Coastal Trail. Follow trail to #890 El Camino Del Mar, and your beginning.

Adolph Sutro bought land in the western part of San Francisco from profits made from the sale of the 4-mile, 1650-foot-deep tunnel he had designed to drain and ventilate the Nevada Comstock silver mines. Sutro was a mining engineer who arrived in San Francisco in 1850 from Aix-La-Chapelle. He was mayor from 1894–1896. His legacy is profound and beneficent. He opened up areas of western San Francisco for the general public to enjoy. He planted trees (while his choice of species was not appropriate for San Francisco, they held the soil, and the trees are gradually being replaced). He founded the Sutro Library and even opened his private property to the general public. He is one of my San Francisco heroes.

Sutro Heights, Sutro Baths Ruins, and the Cliff House are now under the jurisdiction of the Golden Gate National Recreation Area. The GGNRA office in the Cliff House has historic photographic enlargements of the area and also books for sale. A multi-million dollar rehabilitation of the Cliff House restaurant is scheduled to begin in 2001.

In 1865 James Cooke walked from the Cliff House to Seal Rocks on a tightrope.

▲ Part One of the Lands End walk begins behind No. 902 Point Lobos Ave. (Louis' Restaurant at this writing), on a descending footpath. Below are the ruins of Sutro Baths, which were opened in 1896, closed in 1952, and destroyed by fire in 1966. In this eroded sandstone setting, with the offshore Seal Rocks in the background, are broken columns, fragments of tile mosaic, and the emptied pool area extending oceanward. You can often see six or more sea lions on Hermit Rock. (As early explorers approached from the ocean side a distance away, Angel and Alcatraz Islands looked like a continuous horizon line. This explains why San Francisco was discovered via a land route from the south, rather than from the sea.) Continue along the curving path.

▲ Primrose, lupine, poison oak, blackberry, and nasturtium grow alongside the path. Park botanists are cultivating plants native to the sand dunes. Along the way you can see dune tansy, blue bush lupine, beach primrose, and coyote bush. Albizia, the tall shrub with white spiky flowers grows everywhere. It covers the slope next to the 8-foot-wide, railroad-tie Stairway you climb to Merrie Way parking lot. About halfway up the slope on the right, the projected GGNRA Information Center will be built, replacing the one in the Cliff House.

- Turn left at the Merrie Way parking lot and take the lower Coastal Trail. You may soon hear foghorns. Their sounds may be coming from the Golden Gate Bridge, Point Bonita Lighthouse, or Mile Rock (a mile from the middle of the shipping channel, not a mile from shore). Each foghorn has its recognizable pattern—however many seconds of sound followed by seconds of silence. From the right side of the trail you may periodically hear the gurgling sound of water, indicating a seep. Usually, you'll find a patch of green or flowers nearby.

- At the intersection of the Coastal Trail with the Lands End Stairway (left) and one leading up to Camino Del Mar, there had been a series of signal stations, where people were stationed to spot different ships coming in through the Golden Gate. They would then relay the information, first via semaphores and later via telegraph, to the wharf area. (From the left side of the road, crane your neck right to see remnants of the former lookout structure.) Because this area can suffer landslides during heavy winter rains, parts of the trail may be closed. Walk on any alternate path as indicated. (Note the call box beside the trail.)

- As you continue on the lower Coastal Trail, you will see a concrete wall on the right side. It was actually the retaining wall for the Sutro Railroad. Now it's just holding up the hillside. A landslide in 1925

Sutro Railroad, circa 1890

courtesy National Park Service

Lands End

closed off most of the rail lines. Shipwreck spotters liked to come here via the railroad, which came from Presidio Ave. and California along the cliffs. (GGNRA docent Rich Harnett gives a popular shipwreck hike open to the public by reservation, 556-8642.) Most shipwrecks occurred due to some combination of fog, northwest winds, sand bars, and rocky shoals. As you're now in front of the second wall, to your left during low tide you can see remains of an engine block from the wreck of the *Frank Buck*.

▲ During World War II the Army had coastal defenses and gun batteries along the cliff line here and spotting stations at Sutro Heights.

▲ Walk past some serpentine and granite rocks, beyond an emergency call box. To the right is the paved road that goes to the golf course. Painted Rock on your right was a Coast Guard navigational tool. It was used as a sight line with Point Bonita Lighthouse.

▲ Just ahead in the fenced area was the tunnel through which Sutro's train rounded the bend. The tunnel collapsed, the cliff partially fell away, and the trail has been routed uphill—around to the right.

▲ You pass Deadman's Point on the left, and then come to Eagle's Point Platform, which you ascend via a ramp. Eagle's Point once had 28 trees, but 26 of them died because of people trampling on their roots. When the Stairway was built in 1980, the Park Service raised the ground level to protect the tree roots, and fitted railroad ties over them.

▲ There's a good view of Seacliff, China Beach, Baker Beach, the Golden Gate Bridge, and Fort Point. Walk across the platform to the opposite Stairway. Descend as far as you'd like and then return. Continue left to explore the Seacliff neighborhood.

▲ Walk back to the beginning via the upper Coastal Trail. Take the dirt path to your left, almost opposite Eagle's Point. Pass the new location of the Katherine Delmar Burke School, a private girls' school that has been in existence since 1908. The path borders the Lincoln Park Golf Course. On a knoll near the cypress are some of the remains of the 1868 cemetery. More than a thousand graves, many of them Chinese, were discovered when the Museum was retrofitted and redesigned in 1993. It is possible from some places along the walk to see the remaining tall Chinese gate, if you look toward the right. I heartily recommend docent Wolfgang Schubert's walk for the GGNRA, "Legends of Lands End"; for reservations call (415) 556-8642.

- When you arrive at the Lincoln Park Sports Grill, bear right to connect with Legion of Honor Dr. It is an 8-minute walk to the Museum. The Muni No. 18 stops in front of the Legion, if you want to end the walk here. If you wish to see the current exhibit and have lunch in the Legion, do go in (no entry fee for members).

- You can walk around the grounds and explore the views. Walk toward the right near the pool to see the outdoor sculptures—*Pax Jerusalem* by Mark diSuvero, the Holocaust Memorial by George Segal and, toward the left, the Osaka Sister City Commemorative sculpture.

- Continue west beyond the Sister City sculpture along the paved road, which becomes a pedestrian trail after the first stairway. The path leads to the parking lot on El Camino Del Mar (the earlier road had been washed out) where the USS San Francisco Naval Memorial is located. The Memorial is formed from the bridge of this ship that was torpedoed in November 1942 during the Battle of Guadalcanal.

- Above the parking lot, up toward the trees on the left, a semaphore is attached to the Octagon House Signal Station (now a private residence). It was used to relay what ship was coming in, and what it likely contained, to Telegraph Hill and Fisherman's Wharf. When electricity became available, semaphores were replaced by the telegraph.

- You descend the stairway to the right of the Memorial to the lower Coastal Trail, and turn left to reach the Merrie Way parking lot. From there, descend the stairway (right) to the Sutro Baths Ruins. Bear right to the Point Lobos Overlook. The view is a rewarding finale to your walk. Walk toward the left among the Ruins to ascend the incline to Point Lobos Ave. and your beginning.

Further Ambling

Explore the area south along the Great Highway. The GGNRA Visitor Center has information on the various sites within the GGNRA (and posters of the Sutro Baths in the early days). The hiking paths along the Great Highway south of Balboa have been tastefully landscaped for hikers and cyclists (sand control is more successful now than formerly). For a long hike, you might continue to Fort Funston to see the hang gliders and tour the nursery where GGNRA plant seedlings are propagated.

Part Two (*alternate starting point*)

You begin next to No. 890 El Camino Del Mar, in the Seacliff neighborhood. Seacliff was developed in 1924, with curving streets and gateway entrances at 25th, 26th, and 27th Aves. Homes are large, ocean views from north-facing windows are vivid, and gardens on the south side are verdant.

▲ Mark Daniels, former General Superintendent and Landscape Engineer of the U.S. National Parks, laid out the system of curving streets and terraces. (He also designed the street pattern in Forest Hill, Walk 11.) The architect Willis Polk designed three homes in Sea Cliff—Nos. 9, 25, and 45 Scenic Way.

▲ Recollecting his childhood, a former resident of Seacliff remembers walking through the sand dunes, and the seas of gold and purple lupine. Rabbits, snakes, and wild canaries lived in the area then; he remembers his father trapping the canaries and feeding them hard-boiled eggs. He also recalls fishing every other day from Lands End.

▲ El Camino Del Mar was also on the route of the Lincoln Highway, the first transcontinental highway (1915), which began in New York's Times Square and ended here in Lincoln Park. Someone absconded with the plaque END OF THE LINCOLN HIGHWAY, which was once in the pool in front of the Legion of Honor. Hidden on a concrete stand behind the cotoneaster shrubs at the corner of 32nd Ave. and El Camino Del Mar is another plaque: THIS HIGHWAY DEDICATED TO ABRAHAM LINCOLN.

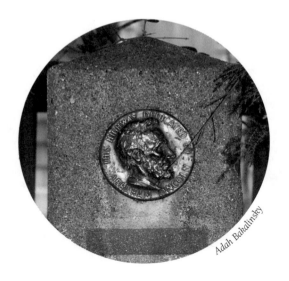

Adah Bakalinsky

▶ Follow the Coastal Trail into Merrie Way parking lot, and turn right to descend the Stairway to the Sutro Baths Ruins. Keep on the path (right) to the large platform at Point Lobos Overlook. As you explore the area, please follow designated paths only. To your left are the former pools, one of fresh water, the others salt. The honeycomb rectangle was the heating plant. Adolph Sutro designed and engineered the structure with its seven indoor pools, each heated to a different temperature. A swim, rental of a suit, towels, and locker cost $0.25. There was room for 10,000 swimmers and seats for 7,000 spectators. The conservatories were decorated with palm trees and Egyptian artifacts.

▶ Walk toward the incline (left) and ascend toward the cliff. At the top you'll be on Point Lobos Ave., behind Louis' Restaurant. Turn left on Point Lobos Ave. to Merrie Way parking lot. Walk through it to the left to find the start of the lower Coastal Trail. Follow this trail to No. 890 El Camino Del Mar and your beginning.

Further Ambling

You could continue to your right on El Camino Del Mar to Seacliff Ave. and China Beach. A stone has been placed at the top of the China Beach Stairway to commemorate the Chinese fishermen who used this site. China (formerly James D. Phelan) Beach is well maintained, with lifeguards, a bathhouse, picnic tables, and benches for watching boats. A longer walk would take you to Baker Beach. Follow the sign at No. 320 El Camino that says PUBLIC BEACH. Turn left on Seacliff and, at 25th Ave., turn left into the cul-de-sac to take the Stairway to Baker Beach. (The Muni #29 bus stop is near Baker Beach. For a full day's outing, continue on El Camino to the Presidio, take Lincoln Blvd. to Fort Point, and continue on waterfront paths around Fisherman's Wharf; see Walk 6.) With almost 4,000 acres of the GGNRA within the City your walking opportunities are boundless!

Lead Thread

GOLDEN GATE HEIGHTS

on a Sugar Sack

The vast tract of land known as the Sunset
District sprawls south from Golden Gate Park to
Sloat Blvd. and from Stanyan St. to the Pacific
Ocean. At one time it was all sand dunes, and a
Sunday's outing to the beach, with lunch or dinner at the
Cliff House on the Great Highway, was a gala occasion.
Silting is a continual problem, but it has been minimized on the
Great Highway by a new design of raised paths for bicyclists and
pedestrians, plus the planting of dune tansy and ice-plants. The outer
Sunset gets wind and fog, magnificent sunsets, the ocean view, and
clear, clean air.

The establishment of Golden Gate Park in 1870 promoted the settlement of the Sunset. Other events continued the process: a railroad was
built along H Street (Lincoln Way) to the beach in 1879; in 1898 U.C.
Medical School was established; in 1904 a Midwinter Fair was held in
Golden Gate Park; and in 1905 St. Anne's Church was founded. The
earthquake of 1906 brought people to the outer lands, away from the
damaged areas of Telegraph Hill, North Beach, and Russian Hill.

Mass housing techniques perfected in the 1920s were utilized by the
three leading contractor/builders in the Sunset: Henry Doelger,
Raymond Galli, and Fred Gellert. The new process enabled them to sell
homes in the late 1930s for $5,000. Construction recommenced in
1945 after the end of World War II. Development of homes with tunnel
entrances, the "Sunset look," where living rooms were built above
garages, solved problems posed by smaller (25' x 65') lots and the low

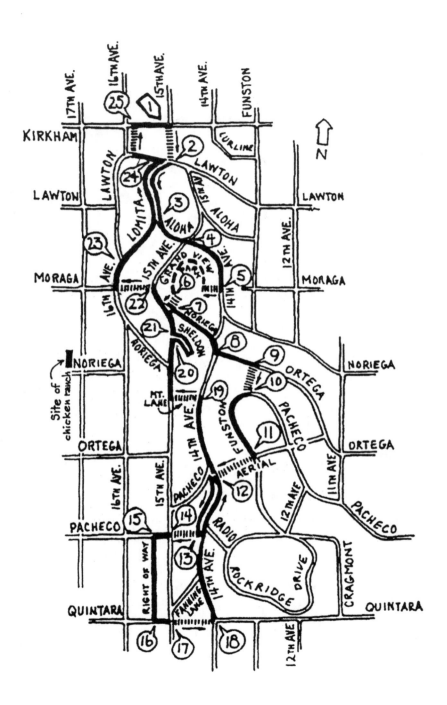

$6,000 ceiling of available FHA loans. Sixty to eighty percent of the homes are owner-occupied.

The Sunset has a stable population of middle-class families from many different ethnic origins, the most recent residents being Asian-Americans. According to the 1990 census, Asians comprise 45%, whites 47%, blacks 2%, and Latinos 6% of the Sunset population.

WALK 10: Golden Gate Heights Route

Public Transportation: Muni #N Judah Metro stops at 15th and Judah. Walk one block south to Kirkham.

1. Begin at Kirkham and 15th Ave. Ascend 15th Ave. Stwy. to Lawton and Lomita.
2. Turn right, slightly. Walk on odd-numbered side of Lomita.
3. Bear left on Aloha at Aloha and Lomita.
4. At intersection of Aloha with 14th and 15th Aves. bear left on 14th. Walk on upper level.
5. Ascend Grand View Park Stwy. on the right. Walk around to the right for the view. Ascend hill along the path. Near the cypress tree, turn right onto the Stwy.
6. Descend to Noriega.
7. Turn left and cross 14th Ave. (No. 1762). Bear right.
8. Turn left on Ortega at the corner of Ortega and 14th.
9. Right on Cascade Stwy. (east side of No. 601 Ortega). Ascend to Pacheco 900 and Funston 1800.
10. Follow Funston to the right. Walk on the odd-numbered side.
11. Descend Aerial Stwy. (next to No. 1895 Funston) to 14th Ave.
12. Left turn on the 1900 block of 14th Ave.; walk along the lower level. At fork of upper and lower 14th Aves., walk on lower.
13. Descend Mandalay Lane Stwy. at the intersection of radio 000 and 14th Ave. 2000. Stairway ends next to No. 1998 15th.
14. Cross 15th (2000 Block). Walk downhill on Pacheco (1100).
15. Left into right-of-way next to No. 1125 Pacheco.
16. Left on Quintara to 15th.
17. Ascend Quintara Stwy. (next to No. 60 Fanning) to 14th.
18. Left on 14th onto upper level.
19. Descend Mount Lane Stwy., next to No. 1795 14th, to 15th. Turn right.
20. Right into Sheldon cul-del-sac, and then return.
21. Right on 15th to No. 1701 15th.
22. Descend Moraga Stwy. to 16th Ave.
23. Right on Lomita to Lawton.
24. Left on Lawton. Next to No. 970 Lawton descend 16th Ave. Stwy. to Kirkham.
25. Right on Kirkham to your beginning.

Golden Gate Heights is one of the neighborhoods of the Sunset. Scouting out the walk was reminiscent of trying to find the beginning loop thread that, with one pull, automatically unlocks the others, opening a 10-pound sugar sack. When I found the lead stairway in Golden Gate Heights, all the other stairways "unlocked" and I felt as if I was on a Matisse walk—just one uninterrupted line with many curves.

▶ Begin this walk at Kirkham and 15th Ave. Ascend the 15th Ave. Stairway next to No. 1501 15th.

▶ Graduated brick sidings edge the stairway. Imagine navigating the long, sloping, open hillside in rain and mud without the stairway! This wonderful artifact not only best promotes easy ascent, but it is also earth friendly, protecting the soil from erosion. Native plants are gradually being restored, but on the upper right slope there are still Himalayan blackberries. Take the 160 steps upward at a slow pace to enjoy the small gardens and the view from each landing. At the fourth landing, you can see the twin spires of St. Ignatius Church to the northeast. At the fifth landing, toward the right, St. Anne's of the Sunset Church is in view, and behind it, toward the right, the Byzantine dome of Temple Emanu-El. Behind you toward the north are the Marin hills and the orange towers of the Golden Gate Bridge, half-hidden by the scalloped tops of the trees in Golden Gate Park. At last you reach the top of the stairway, next to No. 850 Lawton at Lomita (the stop for Muni Bus #66).

▶ Turn slightly right to walk on the odd-numbered side of Lomita, for views between the houses. At the intersection of Lomita and Aloha, bear left on Aloha. At the intersection of Aloha, 15th Ave., and 14th Ave., cross the street and bear left onto 14th, walking on the upper separation.

▶ Ascend the stairway parallel to Moraga into Grand View Park on the right, a superb place to watch the sunset. The 1.1-acre park is habitat for several native plant species: bush lupine, beach strawberry, bush monkey flower, and coyote bush. The rare and endangered plants here are the Franciscan wallflower and the dune tansy. Restoration of Grand View Park is under the aegis of the Yerba Buena chapter of the Native Plant Society and the Natural Areas Division of the City Recreation and Park Department. Both local neighbors and Eagle Scouts participate in volunteer work.

▶ When you reach two wood benches, walk around to the right for the view. You're walking on a hill of windblown sand, but underneath it is chert, layered at odd angles, reddish in color, and imbedded with pieces of radiolarian, the one-cell marine rhizopod. Geologists have found radiolarian hundreds of feet below sea level and have dated samples at 140 million years. Walking near remnants exposed as the ocean receded, you feel connected to the beginnings of time.

▶ Where the footpath is not clearly delineated, walk on the first uphill path; near a mature Monterey cypress, turn right. The gray stumps scattered about look like dune driftwood. Concrete piers support a wood stairway accented by a wood handrail. A very nicely sited wood-slat bench on the landing allows you to look out west over the ocean.

> *I walked along Oxford Street. The buses are strung on a chain. People fight and struggle, knocking each other off the pavement...a motor car accident. To walk alone in London is the greatest rest.*
> —from *The Diary of Virginia Woolf*

▶ Turn right to descend the wood stairway. In the distance Golden Gate Park is a sea of green cutting a swath between the Sunset and Richmond neighborhoods. The curving street that snakes through the park is 19th Ave. St. Anne's Church, a Sunset neighborhood icon stands out like a sentinel. Views to the west feature the Sunset Reservoir and demonstrate the relative flatness of the neighborhood stretching oceanward. Another information placard about Grand View Park is strategically placed at the bottom of the stairs.

▶ Turn left and walk on the upper portion of Noriega. After crossing 14th Ave. (near No. 1751) bear left along the upper section of Ortega. The hill on the corner of Ortega and 14th, also being restored by the Native Plant Society, has an exposed Franciscan Formation outcropping. No. 601 Ortega (1953) is built up on the rock. Before two other houses were built on neighboring lots, it was immediately apparent that this is one of the most dramatically sited residences in San Francisco.

▶ Turn right on Cascade Stairway, an unexpected tuck-in and right-of-way on the east side of No. 601. From the base, Twin Peaks is clearly in view. Walk up to Pacheco beside flourishing gardens. Carl E.

Larsen, a Danish restaurateur, loved this area. His chicken ranch on 17th and Noriega was the site for the annual Easter Egg Hunt for neighborhood children. By the time of his death in 1924 at age 84, he had given the City six acres of land in Golden Gate Heights, including Golden Gate Heights Park.

▶ At the top of Cascade the street signs read PACHECO 900 FUNSTON 1800. Follow Funston to the right, walking on the odd-numbered side for ocean views between the houses. Next to No. 1840 is a redwood house atop the hill; plantings adorn the wood stairway in front. Houses on the odd-numbered side date from the 1970s. Across the street from No. 1886 Funston is the Aerial Stairway, which you descend. One of the longest in San Francisco, the Aerial is surrounded by cypress and ice-plant.

▶ At the bottom of the stairway, turn left on the 1900 block of 14th Ave. Walk on the lower part of this divided street. Succulents, a Hollywood juniper, and daisies, narcissus, and alyssum grow along the retaining wall.

▶ When you reach the intersection of RADIO 000 and 14TH AVE. 2000, Mandalay Lane Stairway is just a few feet farther (the name is inscribed in the sidewalk). Descend the stairway while enjoying the ocean view. Cross 15TH AVE. 2000 and continue down the 1100 block of Pacheco. To the right is Grand View hill and the new stairway you ascended earlier. Walk downhill on Pacheco. The houses on Pacheco are noticeably smaller than those on 15th Ave.

▶ Next to No. 1125 Pacheco turn left into an alley entrance, or right-of-way. Turn left on Quintara to 15th Ave. to ascend Quintara Stairway. It's a double stairway that telescopes at the landing into a single one. Whenever I walk here I visualize a trompe l'oeil painting all the way down the stairway and handrails—and trees with ceanothus ground cover on the adjoining slope.

▶ At the top of the stairs you're at the Bus #6 (Parnassus) stop, on 14th near Quintara. Turn left on 14th onto the upper level, from where you can see ocean breakers. Continuing on the upper level of 14th Ave. (2000), note the rock formation ahead and the stairway you previously descended. No. 1930 14th Ave. (the first house built on this hill, in 1940) is exquisitely landscaped with bamboo, holly, and cypress. A rope handrail and a rock stairway at the entrance are congenial elements in the overall design.

- Now in the 1800 block of 14th Ave., you walk past the descending stairway next to No. 1883. This is the other side of the hill facing Ortega. Just past the mature acacia, a profile view of the chert outcropping on the Ortega and 14th Ave. hill comes into view. No. 1843 faces directly onto the Franciscan rock outcrop. The rock always reminds me of Hawthorne's short story, "The Great Stone Face," where a child spends many hours looking at a rock formation in New Hampshire's White Mountains. One of his favorite stories, related by his mother, was the folk tale of "a child who should be born hereabouts who was destined to become the greatest and noblest personage of his time, and whose countenance in manhood should bear an exact resemblance to the Great Stone Face." He becomes the great stone face. As I reflect on the story, two hawks are circling above me.

- Next to No. 1795 14th you descend Mount Lane Stairway. A neighbor has been gardening with native plants. Halfway down on the right is a swimming pool that looks as if it belongs to a group of houses. "No. 7" is on the gate.

- The stairway ends across from No. 1801 15th Ave. Turn right. Bus #66 (Quintara) runs here. While walking on 15th near No. 1774, detour to the right into Sheldon, a quiet cul-de-sac. Here are the apartments that belong to the swimming pool!

- Return to 15th and turn right to No. 1707. The land in front of you is scheduled for a future park. Next to No. 1707 15th descend the Moraga Stairway. The hillsides need restoration work but the views of the western section of Golden Gate Park and the Golden Gate Bridge are rewarding.

- Turn right on 16th Ave. to Lomita, now walking uphill. At the intersection of Lomita and Aloha there's a triangular section with a small stairway enhanced by shrubs and flowers (the work of a nearby resident). University of California buildings are on the right; behind them is the Sutro Forest.

- Turn left on Lawton (walk on the right side of the street) to descend the 16th Ave. Stairway (next to No. 970) to Kirkham. From the top of the stairs, you can see the Marin hills. Farther down on your right is the 52-story, carnelian granite Bank of America. Turn right to your beginning. (To volunteer for planting and weeding work parties, contact the Golden Gate Heights Association at (415) 566-3984.)

Further Ambling

You could continue north to the intersection of Judah and Irving, friendly, older shopping streets with many individually owned stores and restaurants. Between Judah and Lincoln, 9th Ave. also features rows of specialty shops, restaurants, bookstores, a shoe shop, a video-rental shop that specializes in foreign and cult films, cafe espresso retreats, and a natural-food store.

Marienbad

FOREST HILL

in San Francisco

It's not the longest stairway in the City, or the steepest; not the most charming, or the most personal. Filbert and Vallejo stairways, Oakhurst Stairway, Vulcan and Harry stairways, and Pemberton Stairway, respectively, have these attributes.

However, the Grand Pacheco Stairway is by far the most elegant in San Francisco. An urn of flowers 20 feet in diameter introduces this long stairway placed amidst forest and lawns. The stairs themselves—18½ feet wide, with balustrades, columns, and patterns of stones repeating into the distance—lend a dreamlike, rococo quality to the setting. Think of Alain Resnais' film, *Last Year at Marienbad*, and how easily the Pacheco Stairway could fit the surroundings of Marienbad. This walk of curves and curlicues reiterates the innate elegance of this stairway in its Forest Hill setting.

Forest Hill was originally part of the 4,000-acre Rancho San Miguel, granted in 1843 to José de Jesús Noe, the last Mexican alcalde of San Francisco. After California became independent, the 11 ranchos that comprised the town were subdivided. In 1880 Adolph Sutro bought 1,100 acres of Noe's rancho; the Crocker Estate bought the rest.

Public transportation became easily accessible to the western part of the City after the Twin Peaks Tunnel was built. In anticipation of this, the Newell-Murdoch Company began subdividing the Forest Hill tract in 1912, cutting down much of what had been extremely dense forest planted by Adolph Sutro and his Arbor Day volunteers. Difficult engineering and construction problems were solved in a most esthetic manner by Mark Daniels, the landscape engineer (and former General

Superintendent of the U.S. National Parks), who deserves a plaque commending his design of curving streets that follow terrain contours, generous stairways, ornamental urns, concrete benches, balustrades, parks, and terraces. Forest Hill also has the distinction of having the largest concentration of Bernard Maybeck homes in the City. (He also designed the Clubhouse at No. 381 Magellan.)

No. 266 Pacheco was the first house built in Forest Hill (1913). In 1918, the year the first streetcar went through the Tunnel, the Forest Hill Association was organized. They set home-building standards such as a minimum 1,500-square-foot interior and 19-foot setback from the sidewalk. They taxed themselves in order to maintain the grounds; and because the streets and stairways, delightful and unconforming, did not meet city specifications, the Association was also responsible for them. After years of controversy and court action, the City, in 1978, accepted

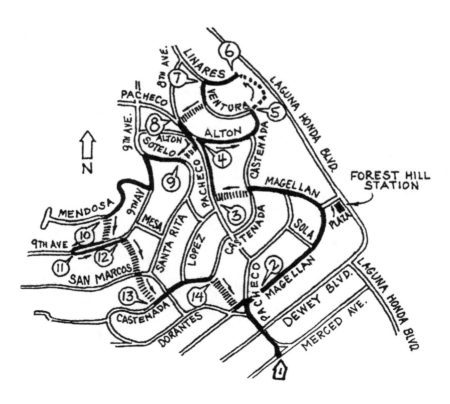

responsibility for streets and curbs in Forest Hill. The residents are responsible for stairways and sidewalks. The Association is still an active community group, which meets regularly at the Forest Hill Clubhouse.

▶ Begin the walk at Merced and Pacheco (technically known as Forest Hill Extension) to experience the gradual change of view—distant to close-up—of the long Pacheco Stairway. The beautiful entrance to the Forest Hill neighborhood is echoed here by the short Pacheco Stairway, with long, curving, concrete benches flanked by griffins on each side, and the large urn in the center green. The fine planning along the axis of Pacheco, north into Forest Hill and south into the Edgehill neighborhood, is unusual in the City.

WALK 11: Forest Hill Route

Public Transportation: Muni L, M, or K Metro to Forest Hill Station. Right on Laguna Honda, and right on Dewey Blvd. to Pacheco.

1. Begin at Merced and Pacheco. Cross Dewey Blvd. carefully to Pacheco and Magellan.
2. Right on Magellan to Stwy. next to No. 140 Castenada. Ascend to No. 334 Pacheco.
3. Right on Pacheco.
4. Right on Alton; left on Castenada to Ventura.
5. Next to No. 95 Ventura, go through open fence to footpath. Walk toward left.
6. Come out of cul-de-sac at LINARES 080 & VENTURA 000.
7. Left on Ventura. Ascend Stwy. next to No. 20 Ventura to Pacheco (No. 452).
8. Left on Pacheco. Walk up 10 steps to upper Pacheco (near No. 400 Pacheco). Continue on Alton Stwy. next to No. 399 Pacheco.
9. At the top of Stwy. next to No. 60 Sotelo, bear right; then left on 9th, and right on Mendosa.
10. Descend the Stwy. between Nos. 91 and 99.
11. Curve right around planted median, then left to Lower 9th (next to No. 2238).
12. Descend Stwy. on lower 9th past San Marcos to Castenada.
13. Left on Castenada to Grand Stwy. next to No. 245.
14. Descend to Pacheco and Merced and your beginning.

Pacheco Street

- Walk north on Pacheco to Magellan; turn right and walk on the right side of Magellan. The trees and the uniform height of the homes provide counterpoint for the variety in the exterior walls, the shapes and materials of the roofs, and the symmetry and coherence, overall appeal, and mellowness of the block. No. 255 is a slate-roofed, brick house, with gardens on three lots, surrounded by a wrought-iron fence, with the finial darts gilded.

- Next to No. 201 is a right-of-way that goes to Dewey. Beyond Sola you soon pass the back of the Forest Hill Muni station. After Plaza you continue to the end of Magellan. Turn left on Castenada to ascend the stairway next to No. 140, a Maybeck-designed house of 1924. The carved grape vines along the eaves (symbol of fecundity) blend in so well with the surrounding vegetation that you almost fail to see this detail. At the top of the stairs, you're at No. 334 Pacheco. Turn right.

- At Alton turn right; then left on Castenada to Ventura. The best weather pattern in Forest Hills is in this northeast section.

- No. 2 Ventura has a magnificent, award-winning cactus garden of many varieties, which complement the southwest style of the house. Veer right into the cul-de-sac. Next to No. 95 Ventura, you go through an opening in the fence to walk left on a footpath. From this 500-foot elevation notice Laguna Honda Blvd. and the reservoir below you.

- Curve around to emerge from a cul-de-sac at LINARES 080 & VENTURA 000.

Samuel Taylor Coleridge walked 10 miles daily and worked out the setting of The Rime of the Ancient Mariner *on a walking tour with Wordsworth.*

- Turn left on Ventura and ascend the stairway next to No. 20, which continues up to No. 452 Pacheco.

- Turn left on Pacheco. Ascend the 10 steps to upper Pacheco (near No. 400). Continue on Alton Stairway, next to No. 399 Pacheco.

- At the top of the stairway you are next to No. 60 Sotelo. (To the left at No. 51 is a 1914 Maybeck house with an off-center, octagonal, pulpit-like balcony; the sides are decorated with shingles and an open carved-wood design.) Bear right on Sotelo, then left on 9th

Ave. to go right on Mendosa. Descend the stairway between Nos.91 and 99 to upper 9th. Turn right to follow the curve around the planted median and arrive at lower 9th.

▶ Descend the stairway on lower 9th (next to No. 2238) past No. 199 San Marcos. You pass a backyard with formal hedges and cobble-stone walls and arches. Turn left at Castenada. Note the 1918 Maybeck, a three-story, shingled residence with bays and dormers at No. 270 (corner of Lopez). Next to No. 245 is the Pacheco Stairway. Descending the Grand Stairway to the street, I think of Jerry Healy, the first superintendent gardener of the tract (also called the "Mayor of Forest Hill"). Healy planted geraniums and marguerites so that the area was a mass of red and white. The Maybeck-designed Forest Hill Club House at No. 381 Magellan can be seen by turning right at the bottom of the stairway. Otherwise, descend to Dewey Blvd. and Merced Ave., and your beginning.

Grading & Sliding,

FOREST KNOLLS

Fog & Drip

Forest Knolls neighborhood is bounded by 7th
Ave. and the Sunset neighborhood on the west,
and by Clarendon and the Twin Peaks neighborhood
to the east. Situated on the south slopes of Mt. Sutro
(918'), it was largely developed for housing in the 1960s.
Though the architecture is similar throughout the curving
streets, the area is rich in geologic history; with alluvial deposits
and layers of sand blown in from the beach over 10,000 years, the
terrain can be instable in times of earthquakes and heavy rains.

After a landslide occurred in 1966, a 10-year building moratorium
was declared. Beneath the layers of sand, Mt. Sutro is composed mostly
of red chert, the dominant rock in the Mt. Davidson/Twin Peaks area.
One of the hardest components of the Franciscan Formation—little
affected by wind and rain—red chert accounts for high elevations in this
part of the City. Yet it can erode into unstable clay. Homes built in the
1980s required expensive engineering to strengthen them against landslide and earthquake damage.

Adolph Sutro, mayor of San Francisco from 1895–1897, loved the
western section of San Francisco. His name is associated with many of
the City's historic legacies: Sutro Baths (Walk 9), Cliff House, Sutro
Library, Sutro Towers, Sutro Forest, Mt. Sutro, and Sutro Heights.
Geographically, Forest Knolls was Adolph Sutro's hunting preserve, part
of his fiefdom of one-twelfth of San Francisco. Sutro (1830–1898) a
mining engineer from Prussia, made his fortune from the sale of the
4-mile tunnel he designed to keep the Comstock silver mines of Nevada
operating safely.

In 1995 two footprints were found in a sandy shore of what was once a steep sand dune, now hardened to gray sandstone, along Langebaan Lagoon near Cape Town, South Africa. Discovered by David Roberts, a South African geologist from the Council of Geoscience, they have been identified as the oldest fossilized tracks ever found of an anatomically modern human. They measure about a woman's size 7 shoe, and have have been dated back 117,000 years.

Because the western section of San Francisco receives significant fog settling in treetops, Forest Knolls became a rain forest after Sutro planted thousands of eucalyptus—as well as Monterey pine and cypress—here and on Twin Peaks to hold the soil. Sutro established Arbor Day

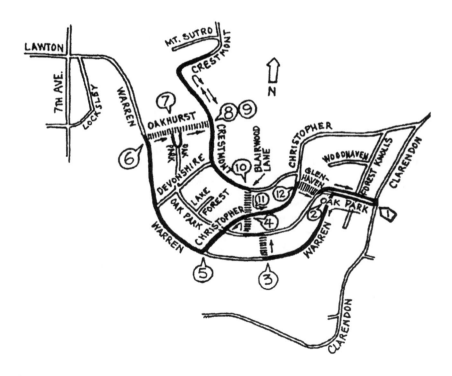

during his term as mayor, and school children participated in planting trees. Today, many of the eucalyptus they planted have been cut or have fallen down—not only have eucalyptus a shallow root system but their life span is 100 years. Yet an abundance of trees still provides habitat and food for many birds, including hawks and owls. Trees also provide a subtle screening among houses, so look closely to see the edifices on stilts, the birds, the ocean, and the elusive stairways.

Residents with whom I've talked express delight in living in a forest, a non-urban section of the City. Yet, a few blocks away they can board Muni to go to a movie, the library, or the store. Not once did anyone mention fog. As you walk along here, you'll enjoy breathing the fresh ocean air.

➤ You begin the walk at Oak Park and Forest Knolls, just off Clarendon. Turn left on Warren. Across from No. 113 Warren is the Blairwood Lane Stairway, which you ascend to Oak Park. Foliose lichen is encrusted on the railings. Lichens flourish where there are no competitive plants and where the air is clean. Vertical gardening is practiced here because of the terrain. I am delighted when I see a successful endeavor. Sedum has been planted on the left among the other vegetation.

WALK 12: Forest Knolls Route

Public Transportation: Muni Bus #36.

1. Begin at Oak Park and Forest Knolls Dr.
2. Bear left on Warren.
3. Ascend Blairwood Lane Stwy. to Christopher Dr.
4. Bear left on Christopher Dr. to Warren.
5. Right on Warren to Oakhurst Stwy.
6. Ascend Oakhurst Stwy.
7. Right into cul-de-sac of Oak Park. Return. Right on Oakhurst to Crestmont Dr.
8. Detour left on Crestmont, and then return to Oakhurst.
9. Continue on Crestmont to Blairwood Stwy.
10. Descend Blairwood Stwy. to Christopher.
11. Left on Christopher to Glenhaven.
12. Descend Glenhaven Stwy. to Oak Park and your beginning.

Forest Knolls

▲ At Oak Park (next to No. 301) cross the street and find a few feet to the left a continuation of Blairwood Lane Stairway. Walk up to Christopher (next to No. 301). The plantings across the street are beautifully terraced with pines, eucalyptus, ice-plants, century plants, and marguerites. To the right you can often see fog hanging in the eucalyptus trees on Mt. Sutro.

▲ Turn left on Christopher. On the slope to the left is a multi-trunked pine covered with lichen. Continue to Warren, and turn right. The attractive, recently-built, single-family dwellings, pastel-colored and angled, thoughtfully allow for maximum light, both reflected and direct.

▲ Across from No. 399 you ascend what I consider a "floating stair-way," the Oakhurst Stairway hidden among eucalyptus. (The *hurst* so often attached to English village names means "wood.") After a slide two years ago, the back windows of the apartment house at No. 401 Warren were covered with mud. Since then, the hillside on the left has been leveled and new drains have been installed. Now the slope is a sea of emerald green grass. You're in a landscape of eucalyptus, bottlebrush, daisies, weeds, ice-plants, and mallow. And the Pacific Ocean extends as far as the eye can see.

▲ The climb is steep. Halfway up the zigzag stairway, you might sit on the steps to admire an extraordinary, wide-angle view as perhaps an ocean liner glides east. Finally at Oak Park, you turn right into a narrow walkway that leads into the cul-de-sac. A series of single-family dwellings have been built on your left. Nos. 560 and 550 were built in 1980, the others in 1990 and 1991. I-beams have been driven deep into the rock to provide safety for these homes, built in this landslide area. Return to the stairs and continue your ascent to Crestmont Dr. Orange lichen on the green hand railings and blue Vinca major, among the variegated greens of ferns, ivy, and eucalyptus, create visual interest near the long retaining wall ahead, which delineates Sutro Woods, Adolph Sutro's former hunting grounds.

▲ Turn left and explore this part of Forest Knolls before proceeding right. Each house on Crestmont has a garden reached via stairs. Between Nos. 95 and 101, near the white fire hydrant, is the Blairwood Lane Stairway. Descend to Christopher and turn left. Just beyond the Glenhaven Lane Stairway (which you'll descend) next to No. 191, you can see the hillside chert outcropping in colors ranging from beige to red. Now walking down Oak Park, you see a monkey-puzzle tree in the distance. Soon you arrive at your beginning.

Further Ambling

Take Clarendon, an important corridor street, to the Twin Peaks, the Forest Hill, or the Golden Gate Heights area. Food is available in the Irving St. and Judah St. sections of the Sunset, or the Market St. and Castro St. sections of Upper Market. At Lawton and 7th Ave. in the Sunset District, you can explore the Garden for the Environment, a demonstration/teaching site for SLUG (San Francisco League of Urban Gardeners).

Angle

TWIN PEAKS, UPPER MARKET, & IRON ALLEY

vs Contour

In the middle of the city is an outcropping of rock, predominantly composed of chert, basalt, shale, and sandstone. It was a daunting task to subdivide the area. Short streets and an interconnecting network of stairways resolved the problem. While the short streets are in many ways comparable to those on the eastern side of the City, these hills are higher than either Telegraph Hill or Russian Hill.

The Upper Market neighborhood is known for its attractive, renovated Victorians, its gardens, and its cooperative neighbors.

▲ Begin at Clayton and Iron Alley Stairway. (It's best to reach this place from Clayton rather than Market.) The street sign at the corner reads CLAYTON END & MARKET 3350. For some reason, the house next to Iron Alley Stairway has a Market St. address: 3304 and 3300.

▲ Ascend the wood stairs, but don't forget to look back. You can identify the former St. Joseph's Hospital, Corona Heights, and the Transamerica building in the distance.

▲ At the top of the stairs you're on Corbett. The new Rooftop School campus for grades K through 8 is across the street. Cross Corbett and continue up the macadam Iron Alley behind the school to Graystone, at the base of Twin Peaks.

▲ Turn left on Graystone, left again on Copper Alley Stairway, and descend the stairs to Corbett. (The views are seen from the odd-numbered side of the street.) Note the view visible through the fence next to No. 579 Corbett. Walk left on Corbett around the bend, past Pemberton, and onto Clayton.

▶ Continue on Clayton to Twin Peaks Blvd. Turn left onto the Blvd. Across the street is a short stairway to Water Department land, where you can walk on the covered reservoir and enjoy an unobstructed view.

If we cross the road, taking care not to be cut down by some rash driver—for they drive at a great pace down these wide streets—we shall find ourselves on top of the hill and beneath shall see the whole of London lying below us. It is a view of perpetual fascination at all hours and in all seasons.
        —from *The London Scene* by Virginia Woolf

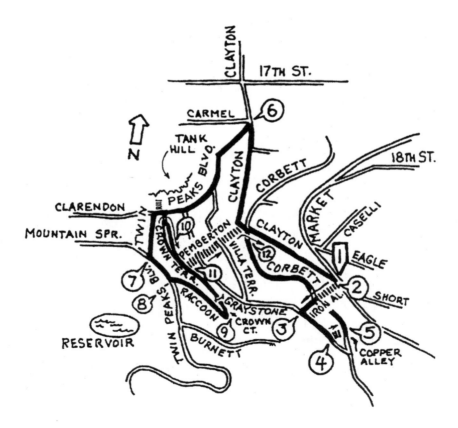

▶ Recross the Blvd. The contemporary house, built according to code but in the face of neighbors' hostility, is at the northeast corner of Crown Terrace. Turn left at Raccoon Dr.

▶ Raccoon offers a spectacular view, unusual for an access road. Continue down to Crown Ct. (open to vehicles). A few homes are sited on the right. Go left, and continue past the stone path and planted area. You are now on Crown Terrace, the pedestrian way.

▶ The stone house on your left (No. 110) is well located in the cul-de-sac. Crown Terrace is part of the district known in the 1930s as Little Italy. The Bank of Italy, subsequently known as Bank of America, held many of the mortgages on the homes (and many of them were foreclosed during the Depression.)

▶ Continue to the end of Crown, then return to the intersection signed 130 PEMBERTON PLACE/98 CROWN TER. to descend Pemberton Stairway.

▶ I enjoy tracking changes in neighborhoods that I have been exploring over a period of years. In 1981 I wrote of that wonderful feeling of luxury I felt the first time I descended the wide section of Pemberton. I thought it was one of the most graceful stairways in the City. The heavy rains of 1982–83 precipitated the deterioration

WALK 13: Twin Peaks, Upper Market, & Iron Alley Route

Public Transportation: Muni Bus #33 (Ashbury).

1. Begin at Clayton and Iron Alley Stwy.
2. Ascend Stwy. to Corbett. Cross Corbett and continue to Graystone.
3. Left on Graystone.
4. Left on Copper Alley Stwy. Descend to Corbett.
5. Left on Corbett around bend, past Pemberton; take Clayton to Twin Peaks Blvd.
6. Left on Twin Peaks Blvd. Cross Blvd., and walk up stairs to see view from reservoir.
7. Return to other side of Blvd.
8. Turn left on Raccoon Dr.
9. Continue bearing left to Crown Ct. Continue left; cross over link chain. You are now on Crown Terrace.
10. Continue toward end of Crown. Return to corner signed 130 PEMBERTON PLACE/98 CROWN TER.
11. Descend Pemberton Stwy.
12. Right on Clayton to Iron Alley and your beginning.

of the brick stairs and the crumbling of the sandstone wall entrance along Clayton. The Department of Public Works installed 4x4 beams to prevent total collapse. In 1991 I wrote that the support beams were still in place. In 1993 cooperative work between the residents and the Department began. In the year 2000 the defective and dangerous stairs were redesigned according to City code: concrete, but terracotta in color and stamped with a brick-shaped mold. New landscaping has been planted: Japanese maple trees at the landing, and shade tolerant ground covers of Vinca major and jasmine, plus colorful annuals. The crumbling wall on Clayton is currently being replaced.

▴ The DPW engineers, landscape architects, and others involved in the Pemberton project enjoyed the challenge of designing a stairway that meets code requirements for safety, as well as the community's esthetic requirements. The teamwork between the City department and the neighbors began with patient and thorough neighborhood grassroots planning, spearheaded by one of the Pemberton residents.

▴ Continue down, past Graystone and Villa Terrace, to Clayton. Across Clayton is the flourishing garden where neighbor volunteers continue the work of the young man who developed the garden but has since died.

▴ Turn right on Clayton to walk to Iron Alley and your beginning.

Further Ambling

If you would like to walk some other little-known short streets and stairways in the area, cross Market at the light, and go to Short, Eagle, and Yukon Streets. To combine this tour with Walk 14, descend the Pemberton Stairway to Clayton. Turn left and go to 17th St. After following directions in the next chapter, end the walk by turning left on Clayton from Corbett and walking to Iron Alley.

Narrow Streets,

Privacy,

& Quiet

If you were to walk from Ocean Beach at the western end of the City and finally arrive at 17th St. and Clayton, you would have worked up to it. After the flats, the land begins sloping up toward 19th Ave. At about 4th Ave. and Parnassus, where the University of California is located, the rise is noticeably higher. At 17th and Clayton, you're even higher, entering a relatively unknown area where cut-off streets confuse, where there is no shopping, and where urban walkers relish exploring. A forty-year resident of Upper Terrace says when people realize how difficult it is to maneuver cars on the narrow street, they usually drive away, leaving behind privacy and quiet.

"I love to annotate the phenomena of the city. I can be as solitary in a city street as ever Thoreau was in Walden"
—from *Sauntering* by Christopher Morley

▶ Begin near the intersection of 17th St. and Clayton. Cross over to the north side of the street (there are apartments at the corner) and walk east down 17th for 50 feet. Now you can see how the apartment complex is sited on the Franciscan Formation outcrop. Return to the corner, and ascend the stairway on the north side of 17th, an abrupt, ambitious beginning, though the rise extends only from 449 feet to 476. Jade plants are growing along the stairway, but through the foliage you can see the Marin hills. At the top you're on Upper Terrace, where multiple dwellings dominate the street.

▲ Turn left toward Monument Way, which at one time marked the center of San Francisco. Bear to the right of the large, circular, raised-concrete planting area in the center of the street. In 1887 Adolph Sutro placed the Olympus Monument here, a sculpture of a Greek

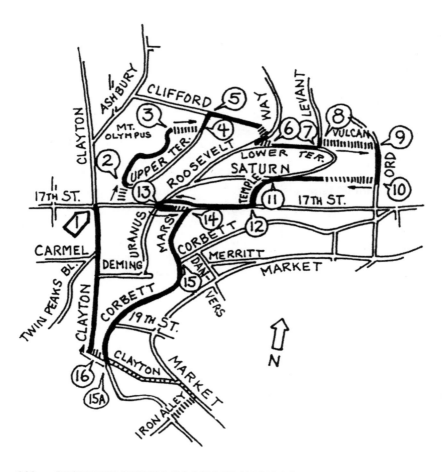

goddess. If you ascend the stairs, you'll see that the pedestal is still present but the sculpture has been removed. The 360° panorama of the City is partially concealed by trees.

▶ Next to No. 480 Monument is Monument Stairway, which you descend to Upper Terrace. A BAY AREA RIDGE TRAIL sign is next to No. 240 Upper Terrace. Turn left. Both the quality of the light and the small distinctive houses make the area feel inviting. Continue on Upper Terrace to Clifford Terrace. Turn right at the bottom of the slope, walk down six steps, cross Roosevelt Way, and descend the Roosevelt Way Stairway.

▶ Turn left on Lower Terrace. Across the ravine is Corona Heights (510'), where native plants have been sowed and new stairways installed to protect them.

▶ Turn left on Levant and, a few feet away, right onto Vulcan Stairway. It was formerly a miniature Shangri-la, where neighbors traditionally worked together to beautify the gardens and walks. The stairway is in a transitional state because some of the older residents are no

WALK 14: Upper Market Route

Public Transportation: Muni Bus #33 stops at 17th and Clayton; #37 runs on Market and Clayton.

1. Begin at 17th and Clayton, ascend Stwy. to Monument Way.
2. Bear left and then right around Monument.
3. Next to No. 480 Descend Stwy. to Upper Terrace.
4. Left on Upper Terrace.
5. Right on Clifford Terrace., descend six steps, cross Roosevelt Way. Next to No. 473 descend Stwy. to Lower Terrace.
6. Left on Lower Terrace.
7. Left on Levant.
8. Right on Vulcan Stwy. to Ord.
9. Right on Ord to Saturn.
10. Ascend Saturn Stwy. to cul-de-sac.
11. Turn left on Temple.
12. Right on 17th to Uranus.
13. Cross 17th, left on 17th to Mars.
14. Right on Mars, walking on upper level to Corbett.
15. Right on Corbett to Clayton.
15a. Left on Clayton to arrive at *Iron Alley (if you are taking Walk 13 also).*
16. Right up stairs to Clayton. Continue right to your beginning.

longer there, and the new residents haven't yet worked out a gardening plan. On one side of the stairs is a row of remodeled, eclectic, mostly turn-of-the-century cottages. Well-designed patios and decks extend outdoor living, and skylights open interiors to natural light. English ivy covers the slopes, and in different seasons fuchsia, rhododendron, azaleas, and hydrangeas are in bloom. New residents of the hill, to whom I spoke, love living here, so I'm sure the gardens will be thriving soon.

▶ At the bottom of Vulcan Stairway turn right on Ord; walk to Saturn Stairway and ascend it.

▶ Visually leading you to the stairway are two, 6'-wide, patterned-brick lanes in place of sidewalks, and sweet fennel and overhanging cotoneaster shrubs on the retaining wall. On either side of center plantings is a stairway—one built of railroad ties, and the other of concrete. Benches positioned on raised brick and header-board platforms let you sit and enjoy expansive views, while nestled in a garden planted with redwood, acanthus, privet, and agapanthus.

▶ At the top of the stairs you enter a cul-de-sac of Saturn, a divided street where you walk along the upper level. The houses are small.

▶ Turn left on Temple. At 17th St. turn right, heading uphill to Uranus. Cross at the stoplight here, and double-back (left) on 17th to Mars. With the 17% grade on this thoroughfare, you can appreciate the difference stairways make in navigating hills. I include a small section on the south side of 17th so that you can better appreciate the land contours, and also walk by some older homes and cottages, which have been here since the 1880s. This area is part of the Eureka Valley neighborhood, which has one of the oldest functioning community organizations in the City. During the 1980s there was extensive renovation of the Victorian homes here.

▶ Turn right on Mars and walk on the upper side. Continue to Corbett, and turn right. A steel gate marks the opening in a retaining wall enclosing the garden at No. 360. Next to No. 377 is Al's Park. The Twin Peaks East Association Community Park continues in the Mono St. right-of-way to Market. It contains fountains, flowers, benches, and fruit trees.

▶ Bearing right, you reach Clayton. (In the first decade of the 20th Century, this was the site of Mountain House Inn. A wood bridge here covered a water run-off originating from Mountain Spring.) Walk up the small stairway. The mini-garden on the side is another

Saturn Street

community project. Market St. is below and the Sutro TV tower is to the left. Don't forget to look back. Continue on Clayton to 17th, walking on the right for Bay views, to your beginning. (If you'd like to end this walk at Iron Alley, you would turn left on Clayton.)

Trees,

CORONA HEIGHTS

Rocks,

& Underground Wiring

This walk takes you on both sides of Corona Heights, which is bounded roughly by Roosevelt, 15th St., States, and Castro. From here you have easy access to the neighborhoods south of Market via Castro and Clayton.

The Corona Heights neighborhood walk has the richness and variety of a satisfying meal. The setting is complex. To the west you see the dramatic rock formation of Corona hill (510'), geologically part of the Franciscan Formation, and very near the City's geographical center. To the east you see the hills, the high-rises, and the Bay. Within the neighborhood you see the shapes and textures of the street trees and individual gardens; the Edwardian houses, ornamented with varied architectural details, and painted in appealing color combinations; the small businesses at street level that provide services and goods for everyday needs—laundries, cleaners, coffee houses, groceries, hardware stores; and a sky unblemished by overhead electric wires.

▶ Begin at the intersection of Buena Vista Terrace and Roosevelt Way. Walking downhill on the odd-numbered side of Roosevelt, you face the Bay. Behind is the large, handsome structure that was St. Joseph's Hospital and now is the 220-unit Park Hill condominiums.

▶ Across the street from No. 26 Roosevelt and next to No. 75, which has a tile plaque of Torre de Belem in Portugal on the right side of the doorway, is the Henry St. Stairway that you descend to the cul-de-sac. Bottlebrush trees delineate the entrance. Two flat, false-front Italianates, No. 215 (1906) and No. 213 (1905), and a pitched-roof with a bay at No. 209 (1906) are of particular interest in this block of Henry.

▶ The hillside, which was cultivated, planted, and tended by neighbors in the cul-de-sac but neglected for several years, is scheduled for renovation and re-design. To your left is the back of McKinley School, a one-story building painted in shades of terracotta.

▶ Cross Castro St. at the stoplight (it's safer) one block left at 14th St. There is also a fine corner grocery where you can buy trail nourishment.

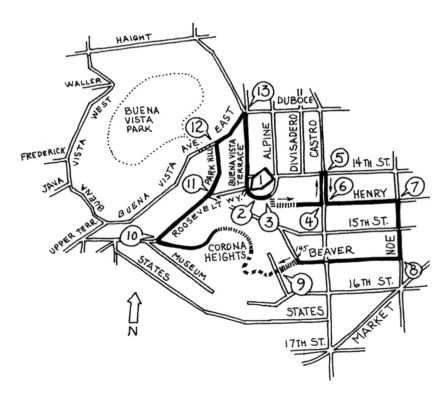

- Go back to Henry and left. No.195 has protruding wires along the roof edge to prevent pigeons from roosting there.

- Turn right on Noe. I particularly like this 100 block because it reflects a village ambiance reminiscent of a New York City neighborhood such as Sutton Place. A strong sense of Nature pervades the street. The green canopies of ficus, carob, gingko, plane, and eucalyptus, together with the variegated colors of impatiens, fushias, daisies, and camellias planted in boxes around small shrubs, create a flourishing environment around the small stores.

- Cross 15th St. and continue to the mini-community garden park at the corner of Noe and Beaver, a felicitous space for friends and neighbors to meet and visit. Turn right on Beaver, where the synergistic effect of a fine assortment of Stick-style Italianates and street trees continues. You are walking uphill. Cross Castro and continue upward. Note the attractive, set-back, two-family home and adjoining garden at Nos. 123–125 Beaver (1879). Next to No. 145 Beaver is the DeForest Stairway. Ascend it to the top, where you'll be at the tennis courts of Corona Heights Park.

- Go through the gate and bear right as you go uphill. Stop for a moment to turn around and look at the Bay, visible between the buildings.

WALK 15: Corona Heights Route

Public Transportation: Muni Bus #37 stops here.

1. Begin at Roosevelt Way and Buena Vista Terrace.
2. Walk downhill on odd-numbered side of Roosevelt.
3. Descend Henry Stwy. to Castro.
4. Left to 14th St.; cross Castro.
5. Walk south to Henry.
6. Left on Henry to Noe.
7. Right on Noe to Beaver.
8. Right on Beaver. Next to No. 145 Beaver, ascend Stwy. into Corona Heights Park.
9. Follow path and stairways to Roosevelt.
10. Right on Roosevelt to Park Hill.
11. Left on Park Hill to Buena Vista East.
12. Right on Buena Vista East to Buena Vista Terrace.
13. Right on Buena Vista Terrace to your beginning.

- You are in back of the Junior Museum, located within one of the most scenic topographical areas in the City—a collection of 200–60 million-year-old chert and sandstone. The Junior Museum is dedicated to Josephine Randall, the first Superintendent of Recreation in San Francisco. She was able to fulfill her dream of establishing a nature museum to instill in children a love of science, natural history, and the arts.

- The Museum is also a popular learning site for adults. It presents lectures, exhibits of geology and anthropology, and classes in natural history, photography, ceramics, and carpentry. It has an important collection of live native animals, the basis for a popular series of talks. (The Museum welcomes volunteers.)

- In its present location since 1951, the Junior Museum has several projects scheduled for completion: a large deck on the building's east side, new landscaping, and a learning garden.

- At the fork in the road/path where the eucalyptus tree stands, bear right on the new stairway. It was installed in 1990 to minimize erosion of the fragile hill and give young native plants an opportunity to take root. Plant-restoration work parties are an ongoing, monthly, volunteer activity. Ahead is a startlingly beautiful panoramic view of the Bay and the hills, downtown San Francisco to the north, and to the south Bernal Heights with its microwave station. You can see McKinley School below to the left, with its striking blue-trimmed vents and red roof. You get a sense of height here, and Corona Hill is a favorite place for rock climbers to practice their skills. A conveniently placed bench is also a perfect station for full-moon viewing. To the left is the former St. Joseph's Hospital. Now continue on the path ahead; the remains of a brick structure are visible as we descend.

> *In 1881 Dr. Ed Livingstone Trudeau, on a bet, walked the length of NYC from Central Park to the Battery in 47 minutes.*

- By following the path fenced along its right side, you reach a clearing adjacent to a dog run. One of the amenities of the dog run is a doggie water fountain. Exit at the gate near the sign JOSEPHINE RANDALL MUSEUM.

- You're at Museum and Roosevelt. (If you would like to visit the Museum, go left on Museum Way for a short distance.) Turn right on Roosevelt. Note the redwood shingle tuck-in at No. 284 (1907), the row Queen Annes at No. 227(1900), and Nos. 225 and 223 (1903). The new town houses across the street are consonant with the ambiance of the block. In addition, the exterior color contributes softness and sparkle to the street.

▲ Continue across Roosevelt to Park Hill. No. 75 has both a living arbor front door entrance, and a living fence.

▲ At Buena Vista East, turn left to see the esthetic Park Hill condos. Note how front and back glass doors are aligned so that the panoramic view through the back door is reflected in the front.

▲ Buena Vista Park, across the street, was so designated in 1870, the same year as Golden Gate Park. It has paths, benches, many trees, various elevations, and many new stairways. It has been undergoing extensive renovation during an erosion-control and reforestation project. (If you have time, amble through now. Otherwise, I heartily recommend you make a special excursion to explore the park.)

▲ Return to the corner of Park Hill to continue on Buena Vista East. No. 181 is an imposing structure on an acre of land with extensive gardens in back. A developer could legally divide the land into five lots. Fortunately, an individual bought the house and lot with the intention of keeping it as a one-family unit. On the balcony ledge, fake owls guard against pigeons. At Buena Vista Terrace, where you see the grand entrance to the park, turn right. Walk past 14th St. to your beginning.

Amazing

Footpaths

Eureka Valley encompasses the area below the southeastern slope of Twin Peaks. Wedged between Diamond Heights, Noe Valley, and Upper Market, it has one of the oldest, continuously functioning neighborhood associations in the City. In the 1920s the composition of the neighborhood was Scandinavian and Irish. The Swedish Church was on Dolores St.; the Scandinavian Deli on Market. John Nurmi's bar at 258 Noe was a great gathering place for the Finnish residents. Schubert's Bakery employed 10 bakers, and was famous citywide for its excellent pastries.

The bakery was the reason that Joseph Affolter's father moved his butcher shop to 2283 Market in 1930—he wanted the overflow of customers from the bakery. Four sons operated the butcher shop for more than 50 years until their deaths. The sign on the wall said DON'T SWEAR. SMILE. Joseph recalled that all meats, including beef stew, were sold with bone in it, and the fillet was part of the sirloin and tenderloin cuts. Families used to shop twice a day for meat and fish.

Eureka Valley's Castro St. (now known as the Castro neighborhood) is the shopping center and hub of the gay community, an important sociological and political force in San Francisco since 1970.

In 1977 Harvey Milk became the first admittedly gay member of the San Francisco Board of Supervisors. (His photography shop and campaign headquarters at 573–575 Castro is now City Landmark No. 227.) After the murder of Harvey Milk and Mayor George Moscone in 1978 by a deranged former supervisor, Harry Britt, who was subsequently reelected, replaced Milk as an openly gay supervisor. The gay movement's militancy created an awareness in the general public of discrimination against gays and lesbians in the police department and in the workplace; it was also effective in influencing the Board of Supervisors to pass the San Francisco domestic partners law, which provides health insurance benefits for the partner of a gay City employee.

Castro Street supports a variety of boutiques, stores, restaurants, and bars. In addition, there is the historic landmark Castro Theatre, a 1922 Spanish Renaissance-style movie palace designed by Timothy Pfleuger (who also designed the Pacific Exchange, 450 Sutter, and the Paramount Theater in Oakland), where revivals of American and foreign films are exhibited, special events such as the gay and lesbian film festivals are scheduled, and an organist plays the Wurlitzer before the first show and during silent features. On the night that Harvey Milk was shot, the Castro Theatre closed and its marquee read IN REMEMBRANCE OF MOSCONE AND MILK.

The gay influence is apparent in many facets of street life: the rainbow banners attached to the light standards; the many skillful renovations of Victorian homes throughout the neighborhood; the taxis generally available; the people carrying bouquets of flowers—as gifts or for their homes; the Twin Peaks bar at Market St., an enduring and highly visible presence for 20 years; the popular Cliff's Hardware (one of the best in San Francisco); the Harvey Milk, the Hibernia Bank, and the Bank of America Plazas where placards and sign-up sheets for various gay causes are circulated. Social services are also available at the B. of A., in an unusual community-cooperative arrangement in which Noah's Bagels pays the rent for the entire building for a specified number of years.

The Eureka Valley walk is a favorite one of mine. More strenuous than some, it has an eloquent cadence of many kinds of stairways; it has paths, alleyways, and skyways. Featuring gardens, tree-lined streets, open spaces, and houses with unusual architectural details, it maintains visual interest through many repeated strolls. Views from it are exceptional. Bring binoculars and perhaps an orange or two (for greater energy).

▶ Begin at Elizabeth and Douglass Streets and walk west on the right-hand side of Elizabeth. You are gradually walking uphill—a perfect introduction to the sidewalk stairway that begins at Hoffman. Abundant and diverse vegetation grows on both sides of the street. The third house from the corner on the 900 block of Elizabeth has lap-board construction; its gate is covered with wisteria and its yard is carpeted with polygonum and Santa Barbara daisies. The residents of No. 970 display a garden of disarming combinations of colors and textures. After crossing Grand View, bear right to the pedestrian overpass above Market, where you have a wondrous view of the eastern half of the City.

▲ Turn right on Market. Next to No. 3801 turn right onto the Dixie Stairway and descend it to Grand View. Cross Grand View and walk down Alvarado to Hoffman.

▲ Turn left on Hoffman to Grand View. Continue to the right on upper Grand View; you'll see a curly leaf willow growing here. Walk past Romain along this divided street.

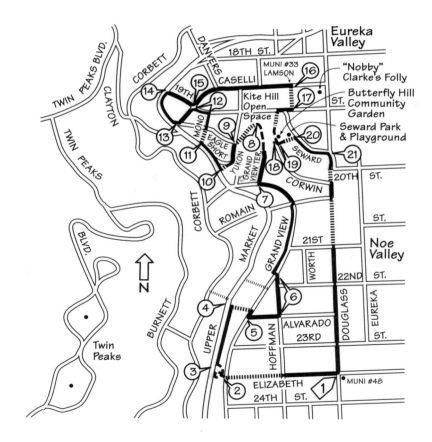

▶ Make a right turn on Grand View Terrace, which leads to Kite Hill. Purchased from Open Space funds, Kite Hill is inviting and functional. Walkers use it, as do dogs and their owners. While sitting on a bench here, I overheard a lengthy discussion among dog owners about dog personality types, while their charges were enjoying playtime.

WALK 16: Eureka Valley Route

Public Transportation: Muni Bus #48 stops at Elizabeth and Douglass.

1. Begin at Elizabeth and Douglass. Walk one block west on the right-hand (north) side of Elizabeth to Hoffman. Ascend the sidewalk stairway to Grand View.
2. Cross Grand View and walk on pedestrian overpass to Market.
3. Right on Market.
4. Right on Dixie Stwy. (next to 3801 Market) to Grand View (across from No. 285).
5. Cross Grand View. Bear right to walk down Alvarado to Hoffman.
6. Left on Hoffman to Grand View. Continue to the right on Upper Grand View (divided street). Pass Romain.
7. Right on Grand View Terrace to enter Kite Hill Open Space.
8. Bear left on second footpath and railroad-tie stairway down to Yukon and Eagle (104 Eagle—to left of street sign).
9. Left on Yukon. Pass Short, taking Short Stwy (with orange-colored railing) to Market.
10. Right on Market.
11. Right on Mono Stwy. to Eagle. Cross Eagle to continue on Mono right-of-way to 19th.
12. Left on 19th to Caselli. Left on Caselli.
13. Right on Eagle to Market; turn right.
14. Right on 19th, facing Kite Hill.
15. Left on Caselli.
16. Next to No. 101 Caselli, ascend stairway to 19th.
17. Cross 19th and continue up the stairway, next to No. 4615, onto a dirt path on the north side of Kite Hill.
18. Follow the left path leading into Corwin and walk to Butterfly Hill Community Garden on the left side of the street; walk down the driveway beside the Garden to Seward Park and Playground.
19. Right on upper pedestrian walkway of Seward to Douglass.
20. Right on Douglass to 20th Ascend Douglass Stwy. Pass Corwin. Walk on pedestrian walkway of Douglass (right side) to Elizabeth, and your beginning.

- On the Yukon St. slope of Kite Hill (toward 19th), the Natural Areas Division of the Recreation and Park Department has been restoring native plants that once grew here. When I accompanied Christopher Campbell of the division in late March, we saw ribes, footsteps of spring, *Lomatium dasycarpum* (wild parsley, a favorite of the anise swallowtail butterfly), *Ranunculus californicus* (California buttercup), *Aster chilensis*, and *Bromus californica*. From the top of the hill there's a triangular configuration of Open Space areas: Tank Hill to the left (west), Corona Heights to the right (northeast), and Kite Hill, where you stand at the apex. At the corner of Yukon and 19th, at the base of the Open Space area, a resident planted a flourishing garden of ginger, echium, and euphorbia, which is counter to the overall native-species restoration of this area.

- Bear left on the second footpath and railroad-tie stairway to Yukon and Eagle. Turn left on Yukon and walk past Short St. No. 25 Short has a garden built under the foundation of Market Street! A young man living there carved niches in the concrete to display sculpture, baskets, and urns. A ceramic cat and a metal sculpture are arrayed along the base of the lower wall beside two chairs. The garden in this most unlikely place—with valerian, roses, dusty miller, curly leaf willow, geraniums, succulents, a spider plant, a redwood tree, fuschia, a lemon tree, abutilon, aralia, and bougainvillea, however in need of pruning—is thriving (a neighbor waters).

- Walk up the stairway to Market, where plantings of valerian and nasturtiums grow along the retaining wall. Turn right and continue beyond Short St. to Mono Stairway.

- Turn right on the stairway to Eagle. Growing alongside are lantana, ceanothus, and rock rose, which has white petals with red targets, indicating the route to the nectar. Cross Eagle to continue to 19th on the Mono right-of-way, with its "archeological" paving mix, consisting of new and old brick, and concrete.

- Turn left on 19th to Caselli, where you also turn left. The resident at No. 303 Caselli has turned an unused city lot into a veritable Shangri-la. The David Austin roses not only look magnificent but their aroma is heavenly. Thirty varieties of birds come here to feed and sing. I was rooted to the spot.

- Turn right on Eagle to Market. Market St. was originally Falcon Road, which later became Corbett, a toll road. Market did not exist west of Eureka St. until the 1920s. Yet, between 1956 and 1958 it was widened to four lanes.

Elizabeth Street

▶ Usually Market is a thoroughfare you drive, so walking here reveals a trove of unsuspected architecture and gardens. On the hill across the street, at No. 3224, is a large pink house (two smaller ones are later additions) on a 90'-deep lot. Known as the Miller-Joost House, it was built in 1867 by Adam Miller, German immigrant, carpenter, and dairy rancher. The house was occupied by Miller's daughter and her husband, Behrend Joost, who built the first electric railroad from Steuart and Market Sts. to the county line in Colma. He also owned the local Mt. Springs Water Co., until the Twin Peaks Tunnel excavation disrupted the flow. The Miller-Joost House has landmark status. (If this piques your interest, see "Further Ambling" later in this chapter.)

▶ Turn right on 19th, where you will be facing Kite Hill. Turn left on Caselli. Near No. 312 the street is edged with cobblestone. At the corner of Danvers a former church is now a private home.

▶ Next to No. 101 Caselli, on the right side of the street, ascend the Lamson Stairway to 19th St. The walkway here is reminiscent of an old-fashioned alley in Chicago. Near No. 4608 19th (top of stairway) cross the street and continue up the stairway beside No. 4615. The dirt section above this stairway leads to the north side of Kite Hill. A bench located here is perfect for contemplating the 135° view of the Bay Bridge. Walk to your left to take in a view of Corona Heights and the downtown skyline, with Eureka Valley and the U.S. Mint in the foreground.

▶ From the bench, follow the path branching into Corwin. On the hillside across from No. 160 is a sculpture of a pelican made of rusty metal. Beyond it, in front of a chert outcrop, is one of a female torso on a stand. The sign across the street reads: WELCOME TO BUTTERFLY HILL DESIGNED AND INSTALLED BY RESIDENTS. Among the beds of 67 native flowers, shrubs, and trees attractive to butterflies are yarrow, mimulus, coyote bush, and mallow. The list is continually growing because the neighborhood project is in-process; the City provides wood chips and water.

> *Mary Walker, 82, of Philadelphia became a walker during a transit strike. She had held down a full-time job at one of the nation's largest banks. After work, she put on her sneakers and took the 7.5-mile walk home. She enjoyed every bit of the walk and saw people racing by, which was not her style. "I get home when I get home."*

▶ Walk down the condo driveway to Seward Park and Playground. With the added benefit of being protected from wind, it's great spot to share a picnic lunch.

▶ Turn right on upper Seward. This elevated pedestrian walkway gives you a better view of neighborhood gardens. Where Seward curves in toward Douglass Stairway, a house and garden (left) faces a hillside (right) planted with cactus, cotoneaster, bamboo, cypress, century plants, and red hot poker. At the top of the stairway look back at the view of Corona Heights Hill.

▶ Cross Corwin and walk up the stairway to the upper level of divided Douglass to enjoy a better view. The Alvarado Elementary School at No. 625 Douglass (at the corner of 22nd St.) has a mural flanking the school entrance, IN MEMORY OF TWO WONDERFUL TEACHERS. Through the initiative and leadership of sculptor Ruth Asawa, Alvarado has had an enrichment art program for the past 20 years. Asawa has used children's art for her public fountains in the Hyatt Hotel courtyard and in Ghirardelli Square. Now, through special funding, her son, a ceramicist, and her daughter, an artist, teach art every day as part of the regular curriculum. The Asawa family tradition has become a community tradition.

▶ The school walls and fence are painted with city scenes, and water scenes with sea creatures. Painted mosaic tiles of a school and bus, and children's heads in a tree, adorn one section of the fence. Children, teachers, and artists participated in a two-year project, which is assembled on a wall in the middle of the school playground. The theme of the 42 x 11-foot ceramic wall mural completed in May 2000 is nature and gardening, and is dedicated to Ruth Asawa.

▶ At the corner of 23rd St. are four, false-gable, rectangular-bay homes to your left. From the middle of the street looking west (in line with the middle of Twin Peaks), you might recall Daniel Burnham's plan for a magnificent viewing corridor from the Ferry Building to Twin Peaks. The 1906 earthquake, and subsequent hurried rebuilding, prevented his 1905 San Francisco City Beautiful plan from being implemented. Continue to Elizabeth and your beginning.

Further Ambling

Alfred "Nobby" Clarke's Folly at No. 250 Douglass, at the corner of Caselli, is a Queen Anne mansion with landmark status. Built on a 17-

acre lot in 1892 for $100,000, it was composed of 5 stories, 45 rooms, 52 closets, 10 fireplaces, and 272 windows. Clarke's Folly today contains 15 one-bedroom apartments.

Clarke was an Irish sailor who immigrated to California in 1850. Beginning his career as a gold miner, he later worked in the Police Department, became a lawyer and, finally, an entrepreneur. The springs flowing from Joost's property in upper Twin Peaks followed the north side of Caselli St. to Clarke's holdings. Becoming dissatisfied with Joost's water service, he started Clarke's Water Works, but in 1896 he went bankrupt.

A Mondrian

DOLORES HEIGHTS

Walk

A good walk is an organism of mysterious nuances that can affect us in subtle ways, from quiet harmoniousness to ebullience, from languor to exuberance. Within a walk for a stamp, a loaf of bread, a bit of exercise, or a breath of fresh air are the promising ingredients of an imaginative walk that charms and delights: the various terrain to step over, the spectrum of sky colors to see, the views of manufactured objects to comprehend, the assortment of people to meet, and the intrinsic rhythm and shape of the walk to sense.

I love to trace out the shape of a walk on paper after I walk it. I want to know if there is a correlation between the shape and how it feels when I walk; there is. For some reason that I don't understand, my early walks usually traced into the shape of a foot or a shoe, and the walks felt very comfortable. Now my walks seem to form fanciful figures, or geometric, Mondrian configurations, and they feel effortless. The Dolores Heights walk is Mondrian choreography!

▶ Begin at 19th and Sanchez. ceanothus, bottlebrush, and acacia grow at the base of the imposing wall flanking the double stairways going up Sanchez. (The first inspection is recorded in 1939.) We ascend the left stairway. A large home at the top, No. 615 Sanchez, replaced a small house. The four cypress trees in front of the house are over 50 years old. At one time Sanchez had brick paving, but it was too slick and had to be covered with asphalt.

▲ Approaching the Cumberland/Sanchez intersection, I was impressed that after 25 years it is still one of my favorite corners in San Francisco. I think it is the combination of houses and trees, a feeling of neighborliness that pervades the street, the configuration of the two streets affording a close-up view and a distant view, and the surprise of seeing all this at the end of the first ascent. Continue walking on lower Sanchez. A few feet farther on, you can see the section of the Cumberland Stairway that goes down to Church. At No. 650 Sanchez (at Cumberland) Cape jasmine and trumpet vine grow under the veranda. Penstemon, valerian, mimulus, rosemary, and acanthus brighten the block, adding their charm.

▲ In front of No. 655 Sanchez, descend the stairs to the pedestrian walkway. At No. 674 Sanchez, New Zealand flax grows behind the rock. You're walking south toward 20th St. on the lower part of the divided street. A center strip of flora and unusual tilted stairs divides the upper and lower parts of Sanchez between 20th and Liberty. The

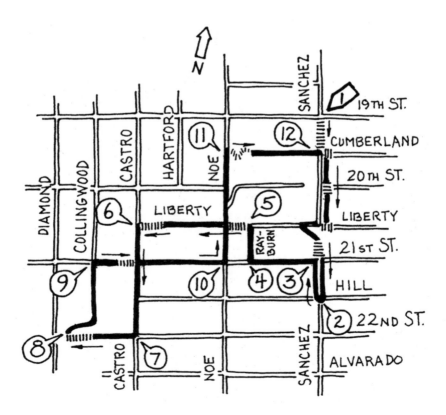

cul-de-sac of Sanchez angles to the left. Ascend the stairway to the right that brings you to the upper level of Liberty and Sanchez.

➤ Cross Liberty to continue up the Sanchez Stairway, which is fronted by a high retaining wall. When you look east (left), you can see the dome of the Christian Science Temple on Dolores St. The redwood-shingled house on the corner, No. 746 Sanchez, conforms to the irregular-shaped lot in a comfortable way; it stretches around the corner. The off-center, arched veranda or possibly carport (although there is a garage off to the side) leads the eye to the terraced garden, where camellias and a mature Douglas-fir are the dominant plants.

➤ Continue to 21st St. The house at the corner, No. 3690, formerly belonged to "Sunny Jim" Rolph, the popular San Francisco mayor (1912–1931). John McLaren, who was the superintendent of Golden Gate Park for 60 years, planted the Monterey pine trees around the house. At No. 3701 21st St., on the southeast corner, a sculptured redwood bench is inset on tile, and dedicated to Audrey Penn Rodgers by friends, relatives, and neighbors. She was president of the Dolores Heights Improvement Club for many years, and diligently watched over the area to make sure it retained its unique neighborhood ambiance.

The swiftest traveler is he that goes afoot.
—Henry David Thoreau

WALK 17: Dolores Heights Route

Public Transportation: Muni Metro J runs on Church with stops on 18th and 20th; walk one block west to Sanchez.

1. Begin at 19th St. and Sanchez. Ascend Sanchez Stwy. to Cumberland; descend small Stwy. to lower Sanchez; return to Upper Sanchez via Stwy.; cross St. Ascend Stwy. from Liberty to 21st. Continue to Hill St.
2. Return on Sanchez to 21st.
3. Left on 21st to Rayburn.
4. Right on Rayburn to Liberty.
5. Left on Liberty. Descend Stwy. to Castro.
6. Left on Castro to 22nd.
7. Right on 22nd. Ascend Stwy. to Collingwood.
8. Right on Collingwood to 21st.
9. Right on 21st. Descend sidewalk Stwy. past Castro to Noe.
10. Left on Noe to Cumberland.
11. Right on Cumberland; ascend Stwy. to Sanchez.
12. Left to descend Sanchez Stwy. to 19th and your beginning.

▲ Walk toward Hill St., formerly called "nanny goat hill" in reference to the goats that grazed here, and enjoy the view to the south. At the turn of the century, the designated neighborhood voting place was a small structure on the top of the hill (right). Before the streets were paved firemen, who were attached to the 22nd St. firehouse between Sanchez and Noe (now a residence), left their pumps up here on the hill as a kindness to their horses.

▲ With so many springs in the area, the Native Americans who once lived near Mission Dolores came up here to get their water. There are still some houses in the neighborhood that have their own capped wells.

▲ Historically, working-class people have resided in Dolores Heights, but now many professional people live here, and the mix enriches the neighborhood. The residents love the sunny, fog-free weather.

▲ At Hill and Sanchez look left to take the full measure of the elevation. Retrace your steps on Sanchez to 21st and turn left. Turn right on Rayburn, which takes you out to Liberty. After a left turn, you soon reach the Liberty Stairway, which you descend to Noe.

▲ Four, white, stucco Art Deco houses alongside the stairway are foils for the multitude of neighborhood Victorians, from elaborate Queen Annes of the late 1880s and 1890s to one-story, flat-front Italianates of the 1870s and early 1880s.

▲ Walking in the neighborhood, I was captivated by the constantly shifting cloud cover playing with the TV tower on Mount Sutro, obscuring it one minute, uncovering it the next. The entire tower is almost visible...

▲ Cross Noe and walk on the left (south) side of Liberty. The 500 block of Liberty is exquisite with small Italianates. Corona Hill with its scooped skyline and the Buena Vista condos to the west, and the Financial District high-rises to the east come into focus; and in close-up you can see a plane tree in front of No. 521 Liberty, and a mature hibiscus across the street. Nos. 564–576 Liberty were built in 1897 by Fernando Nelson, a prolific developer of tract Victorians in this and other Mission neighborhoods. These houses display his favorite wooden embellishments: the decorative circles and pendants that he styled "donuts" and "drips."

▲ Continue on Liberty to Castro, where you turn left. Queen Anne row houses are on the west side (right side, even numbers) of the 700 block of Castro. (Look for the donuts and drips.) Walk to 22nd St.

Sanchez Street

and turn right. This section of 22nd is a turnabout; a sculptural, high-curved retaining wall encompasses the stairway you now ascend to Collingwood. (The stairway beyond it goes down to Diamond.) You're at the top of the hill of this five-block-long street.

▲ Turn right on Collingwood. In 1932, a German mason built the cobblestone house at No. 480, using stones from the dismantled Castro cable car line. Turn right on 21st, which used to be extremely steep from Diamond to Castro. In 1924 the City "improved" the street by lowering the grade on one side while raising it on the other, resulting in a grade-separated street and some non-functioning garages. The one at No. 3937 was converted into living space. Walk down the sidewalk stairway on the odd-numbered side of 21st and continue to Noe. The 3800 block of 21st has an exceptional selection of row Queen Anne Victorians. On the left side, they gently follow the slope of the hill. John Anderson, a contractor, built Nos. 3816–36 in 1903 and 1904. Your view from here includes the top one third of the TV tower.

▲ Turn left on Noe. At Liberty, look right to see the stairway you have previously descended. From No. 741 (on the odd-numbered side of Noe), you can see the skyline to the north and west. Continue on Noe past the curved retaining wall of 20th St. and the narrow stairway alongside the apartment house at No. 695. The houses on the even-numbered side of the street have the potential of becoming a showcase like those on Alamo Square, or on Clay St. across from Alta Plaza Park. Three quarters of the ubiquitous Sutro tower is still in sight.

▲ Ascend the Cumberland Stairway across from No. 670 Noe. The retaining wall, made from cobblestones, is a backdrop to the rock outcropping upon which the stairway was built. Several century plants, set into the rock soil, form a strong upright profile against the jumbled Franciscan Formation. Sedum, gazanias, and ivy are growing here and there.

▲ From the cul-de-sac entrance at the top of the stairs, you begin a pleasant walk alongside tree-lined houses. The Dolores Heights Special Use District, which runs from Cumberland to part of 22nd between Noe and Church, was established 30 years ago to provide residential-design guidelines and preserve front gardens. No. 367 has an octagonal belvedere, roofed in a pattern of blue and lavender tiles. On the cobblestone terrace of No. 338 Cumberland, goldfish swim in the pond. The exterior of No. 333 is cement composition board, a relatively new material being used in San Francisco. The house provides contrast and a contemporary link to the Victorian architecture in the neighborhood. No. 332 is a simple Craftsman-style house. No. 300 is made up of two 1906 refugee cottages, which were originally located in Dolores Park. Known as bonus-plan cottages, they provided affordable housing to those who lost their homes in the 1906 earthquake and fire. (The Finance Relief, the Red Cross, and the U.S. Army originally funded the project.) The Carpenters Union, Local 22, built 5610 shacks. In 1997, 17 shacks were still extant.

▶ Continue to Sanchez, arriving at my favorite corner of Cumberland. Turn left and descend the Sanchez Stairway to your beginning. Places to eat are plentiful along Castro, 18th, and Market.

From Ship Building

POTRERO HILL

to Dot-Com

Geographically, the Potrero Hill neighborhood
is bounded by 16th St. to the north, Cesar
Chavez to the south, Alabama to the west, and San
Francisco Bay to the east. Highways 101 and 280 are
like cradling parentheses. Composed mainly of serpentine
rock, Potrero Hill (300') commands encompassing views of
the City. Climatically, Potrero Hill has some of the best weather
in San Francisco because the larger hills to the west shelter it from
winds. Sociologically, it is known for its strong sense of community,
and its ethnically and racially diverse population.

When the Spaniards arrived in the 18th Century, Potrero Hill area
was a peninsula with its original shoreline intact. It was also pasture
land (*potrero* means "pasture" in Spanish). Horses, cows, and goats
grazed the hill during the Spanish and Mexican period. In the latter half
of the 19th Century, industry located here because of the proximity to
water. Union Iron Works was one of the largest builders of steel
steamships and men-of-war. It later became Bethlehem-Todd. Baker and
Hamilton's warehouse was here in 1849; the site is now occupied by
Show Place Square and the Galleria Design Center. Tubbs Cordage was
in business in 1859, and Tubbs St. is listed on the maps.

Workers for these industries came from Ireland, Scotland, and the
Balkans. 22nd St. and Illinois is the former site of Irish Hill; Scottish
shipbuilders mostly lived on Connecticut. Greeks and immigrants from
eastern Europe seemed to congregate near Mariposa and Vermont.
Boardinghouses for workers were along Illinois and 3rd; cottages along

Tennessee cost $585. In the early 1900s a contingent of White Russians settled around Carolina near 20th.

Because Potrero Hill was unscathed by the 1906 earthquake and fire, people from destroyed areas migrated here. The tent city, official Relief Camp No. 10, extended north to Mariposa, south to between 20th and 22nd, west to Indiana, and east to Kentucky (now 3rd). In March 1907 the tents could be turned in for cottages at a cost of $6 per month. Renters could move the cottages to their own lots. There are four "earthquake" shacks in the neighborhood: Nos. 641 and 649 Arkansas, and Nos. 910 and 922 Carolina.

Good weather, good transportation, and available lots at good prices attracted professionals and artists to the area after World War II. The picture in 2000 has changed. The dot-com influx has resulted in limited available housing plus exorbitant rents and purchase prices.

The walk begins in front of the Potrero Hill Neighborhood House, 953 De Haro at Southern Heights, the focal point for the community since 1907. It was founded by the Presbyterian Church Women's Group to help immigrant groups learn English and cope with changes in their everyday lives. Located in a Craftsman-style landmark building (No. 86) designed by architect Julia Morgan, NABE (the community name for Neighborhood House) has been located on De Haro (a perfect spot for full-moon viewing) since 1922. With Head Start classes ongoing here for many years, NABE provides space for community organizations' meetings and a variety of classes for young people, including art and drama. The community newspaper office is here. Ruth Passen has been the volunteer editor of *The Potrero View* for 26 years. Enola Maxwell has been the director of NABE since 1972.

NABE is both the beginning and the pivotal point in your walk. From here you have a continuous view in every direction. Orient yourself before proceeding on the walk: to the north you get a close-up view of the downtown skyline; east, the Bay Bridge and Yerba Buena Island; south, Candlestick Hill; southwest, San Francisco General Hospital; and west, Twin Peaks.

▲ From NABE on De Haro, walk south along Southern Hts., curving left to 22nd St. Turn left. There's a great view (left) at the crest of the hill. Pass the water tower and the arresting, serpentine rock formation across the street, on which a Monterey cypress grows. As you continue toward Wisconsin, note the two earthquake shacks, Nos. 922

and 910, to your left. Descend the 22nd St. Stairway to Arkansas. Nos. 649 and 641 are two more earthquake shacks on the left. A Bay view stretches before you.

◣ Continue along the path. A Community Garden is to your left, and the PG&E power plant and a mini park is on your right. Turn left on Connecticut. The architectural mix, including several Stick-style homes built in the 1880s (Nos. 512–18 and No. 524–26) on the 500 block, and the variety of street trees are pleasing.

◣ Turn left on 20th St. The Potrero Branch Library is across the street at 1616 20th. The Library has a neighborhood archive collection,

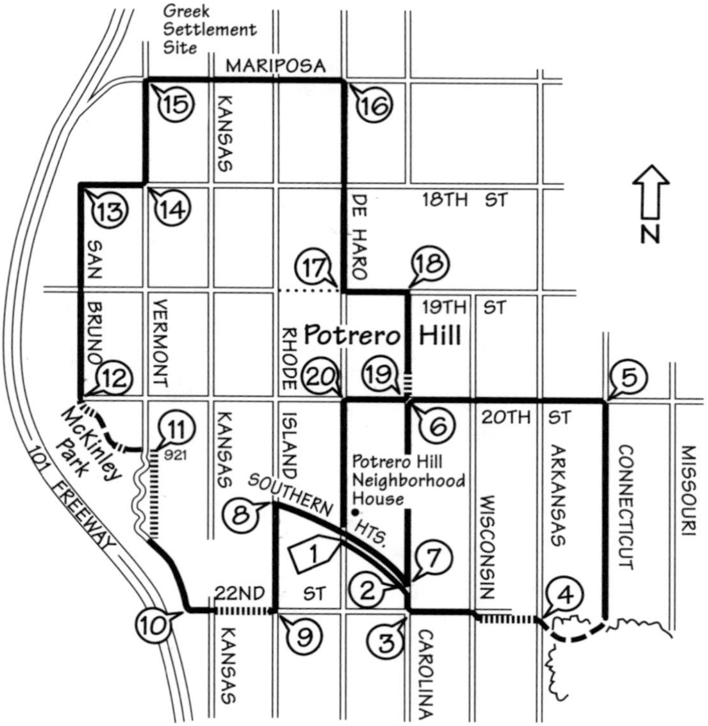

popular reading programs for children, and lectures for adults. Continue to Carolina and turn left. Walk on the right side of the street in order to better view the large serpentine outcropping upon which structures have been built. When you're almost opposite the Molokan Christian Church, walk up the stairway.

▲ When you reach Southern Hts., turn right, curving along it to Rhode Island. Turn left on Rhode Island. As you walk downhill, notice on the right some cottages situated near the back of the lots, the "tuck-ins." These were built around 1910. On the left, houses are built high on the hill. Next to No. 949, you can see the radio antennae on

WALK 18: Potrero Hill Route

Public Transportation: Muni Bus #19 (Polk); #53 (Southern Hts.); #48 (24th St.).

1. Begin at De Haro and Southern Hts. (from NABE at 953 De Haro).
2. Walk east on curve of Southern Hts. to 22nd.
3. Turn left on 22nd and descend 22nd St. Stwy. to Arkansas.
4. Walk along path and turn left on Connecticut; walk to 20th.
5. Turn left on 20th to Carolina.
6. Turn left on Carolina to Southern Hts.
7. Curve right on Southern Hts. to Rhode Island.
8. Turn left on Rhode Island to 22nd.
9. Turn right on 22nd and descend 22nd St. Stwy.; bear right past Kansas to Vermont.
10. Turn right on Vermont. Across from No. 921, enter cul-de-sac (with sign DO NOT ENTER) to ascend Stwy. At first landing, turn left on dirt path. At second landing, turn right, then left to ascend Stwy. to McKinley Park and Playground.
11. Bear left on path around park (past sandbox). Descend Stwy. at corner of San Bruno and 20th.
12. Walk along San Bruno to 18th.
13. Right turn on 18th to Vermont.
14. Turn left on Vermont to Mariposa.
15. Turn right on Mariposa to De Haro.
16. Turn right on De Haro to 19th.
17. Turn left on 19th to Carolina.
18. Turn right on Carolina. Ascend Stwy. to 20th.
19. Turn right on 20th to De Haro.
20. Turn left on De Haro to your beginning.

Mt. San Bruno. Bernal Hts., with its antiquated microwave station, is on the rise to the right of Mt. San Bruno. Silhouettes of the hills are clearly delineated.

▲ Turn right on 22nd and go down the short, steep 22nd St. (side-walk) Stairway. Pass Kansas, and bear right on Vermont. On the slope to your right, agave, morning glory, and cypress trees are growing; they could use some judicious pruning. A sound wall on the left mitigates the heavy traffic noise of the 101 Freeway.

▲ Across from No. 921 Vermont a sign to the cul-de-sac reads DO NOT ENTER. But you enter, and ascend the stairway leading toward McKinley Square Park. At the first landing, turn left on the dirt path. Below you swirls the steam column from the City Hospital laundry. At the second landing, turn right and then left up the stairway into McKinley Square Park at the top.

William Wordsworth walked 14 miles a day in his beloved English Lake District, an estimated 185,000 miles in his lifetime.

▲ Curve around the walkway to the left. When I was here, a gentleman was working at the redwood table under the cypress, and dogs and their owners were using the designated dog run. Renovated and redesigned by landscape architect, John Thomas, the park was dedicated in September 1999. When the Mayor gave the signal, a group of neighborhood children snipped the official ribbon. The new playground is colorful and attractive to children who enjoy exploring the various shapes of play equipment. New benches are very convenient for picnicking and enjoying views, which give youngsters a great opportunity to identify landmarks.

▲ Beyond the large sandbox you descend the short stairway at the corner of San Bruno and 20th St. To the west are the condos on Diamond Heights, the cross on Mt. Davidson, Twin Peaks, and the TV tower on Mt. Sutro. On top of the low retaining wall along the sidewalk at San Bruno and 20th St. is a brass United States Geodetic Survey reference mark, which was placed here in 1932. Cross San Bruno to look at the flourishing Potrero Hill Community Garden.

▲ Continue north on San Bruno. Sunbursts adorn the three gables on the house next to No. 711. The block has flat-front Italianates, many of them redone with "misguided improvements," as Judith Lynch so aptly described them. Street trees are missing on this block. A shingled building, No. 636, has pleached ficus street trees in front and around the corner. No. 619, built in 1913, and No. 609, built in 1910, are some of the older homes in this section. A mini park, THE BENCHES, is located at 18th St. You also enjoy a view of Twin Peaks from here. (A skywalk extends across the 101 Freeway.)

▶ Turn right on 18th St. and left on Vermont. The Slovenian Hall is at the corner of Mariposa where you turn right. The early Greek settlement was in this section. Light industry and small entrepreneurial firms are located in the lowlands north of Mariposa, to your left. There are some dot-com enterprises on Vermont.

▶ Continue east on Mariposa toward De Haro. On your right, an impressive copper gate with a dragon-shaped cutout leads to a parking court belonging to the Episcopal parish of St. Gregory of Nyssa. This cedar-shingled structure was designed by architect John Goldman, and was completed in 1995. The main entrance is at the corner at 500 De Haro.

▶ St. Gregory parish places strong emphasis on liturgy that is grounded in Jewish and early Christian practice. Their belief in unconditional hospitality, a strong sense of community, and in music and dance, is expressed in the shape of the entrance—a large, octagonal open space, with an encircling wall mural of joyous dancing saints. After the liturgy in the adjoining room, the congregation reenters the open space and dances, reflecting the movements of the saints. A table is set with food for all to partake.

▶ Across the street at 1705 Mariposa is the new home (1979) of Anchor Steam Brewing Co., one of the finest small breweries in the country. Its history goes back to the 1860s when it brewed one beer that was available only on tap. Now, under the leadership of Fritz Maytag, Anchor produces six hand-crafted beers. (Tours are available during the week by reservation.)

▶ Turn right on De Haro toward 19th St. You pass Potrero Hill Middle School of the Arts at 655 De Haro, and soon after an open space that contains remnants of a garden. You can see the cantilevered section of the Bay Bridge from here.

▶ Turn left on 19th St. to Carolina, and then turn right on Carolina to ascend the Carolina Stairway to 20th St. At the top are redwoods. The right-of-way has evolved into a garden with trees, agave, ivy, and shrubs. The Victoria Mews Association maintains the garden.

▲ Turn right on 20th St. to De Haro. A large embankment of serpentine rock with plantings is at the southwest corner. De Haro's adobe
cottage was built here in the 1830s. Francisco de Haro was the first
Mexican Alcalde (or "mayor" in 1834) of San Francisco. Walk on the
left side of De Haro in order to have a better view of the new architecture on the right. (Look back for a view of the Bridge.)

▲ Continue walking south on De Haro, past the new mini park in
progress—where a crimson king maple tree has been planted in
honor and memory of Ruth Davidow, a neighborhood activist—to
your beginning.

Stairway

Trails

Bernal Heights sits high above a maze of major
thoroughfares—Alemany, Mission, and Cesar
Chavez streets, and highways 101 and 280. It is part
of what was once the Rancho de las Salinas y Potrero
Nuevo, granted to Jose Cornelio de Bernal in 1839 by the
Mexican government.

In the 1860s the rancho (one league square, approximately
4,000 acres) was subdivided and Vitus Wackenreuder made a survey of Bernal Heights. Wackenreuder plotted his streets narrow and
his lots small: 23 by 76 feet. Most of them do not meet today's City
specifications of minimum size. The east slope exceeds 45-percent grade
in many places, and its geological composition has hazardous landslide
potential.

After subdivision, the first group of settlers was predominantly Irish.
They farmed the land and engaged in dairy ranching, the first extensive
industry in Bernal Heights. Wakes were the most popular social gatherings, along with the telling of stories by "them as had the gift." The day
Widow O'Brien's best milk cow was taken to the city pound and all her
neighbors helped her get it back provided a true neighborhood story,
endlessly told.

German and Italian settlers followed the Irish. During World War II,
there was an influx of people, mainly blue-collar, from all over the
United States, who came to work in the nearby naval shipyards.

More recently professional and media people have been moving into
the neighborhood, attracted by the sunny climate and the neighborhood
ambiance of the village within the City. Since 1995, the east slope of

Bernal Heights has experienced fundamental and dramatic changes. A capital improvement project from sales tax monies has brought the streets into compliance with mandated safety codes. But, along with streets and water lines, the area now has six new stairways (with more to be built) in unused rights-of-way, on hills too steep to construct a street. The stairways at Brewster, Mayflower, Joy, Faith, and Rutledge

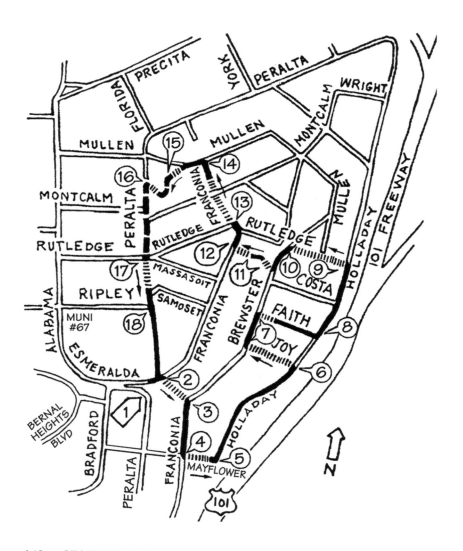

have been renovated and brought up to code, and they now provide safe access to adjoining streets. (Five more stairway projects are planned for 2001.) The Department of City Planning coordinated all this construction, including the approved underground utilities for the East Slope of Bernal Heights. The East Slope is now one grand forest of stairway trails to explore. I encourage you to try out new routes.

The streets of Bernal Heights East meet at angles that vary from the rectangular grid. Also, street names can flip-flop within a block, and several streets converge at a "corner." I have mentioned these facts to several residents, who seem surprised. But they understand the system.

WALK 19: Bernal Heights East

Public Transportation: Muni Bus #67 (begins run from 24th and Mission) stops at Ripley and Bernal Heights; walk one block.

1. Begin at the corner of PERALTA 600 and ESMERALDA 1000.
2. Veer right to descend the (unmarked) Esmeralda Stwy.
3. Turn right on the 400 block of lower Franconia; continue to the right.
4. Turn left to descend the (unmarked) Mayflower Stwy.
5. Walk left on Holladay to Joy Stwy.
6. Turn left to ascend Joy Stwy. to Brewster.
7. Right on Brewster to Faith Stwy. Descend.
8. Left turn on Holladay.
9. Ascend Rutledge Stwy. beyond the Mullen cul-de-sac to Brewster.
10. Left on Brewster (past the retaining wall).
11. Bear right up the Stwy. to entrance of Miller Memorial Grove/Dogpatch Garden. Continue left. Walk through community garden.
12. Right on Franconia to Rutledge.
13. Descend Franconia Stwy. to Mullen.
14. Left turn on Mullen. Ascend the ramp Stwy.
15. Follow the path.
16. Turn left on Peralta path and left again to follow garden path.
17. Next to No. 402, ascend the Peralta Stwy.
18. Continue on Peralta past Ripley, to the beginning of your walk.

- Begin at the "corner" of PERALTA 600 and ESMERALDA 1000. Across the street is the unmarked Esmeralda Stairway, which you descend. New landscaping and new amenities set the tone for an adventure along the recently improved Bernal Heights stairways. You'll see plum trees and pines, and various annuals. New fixtures include improved lighting and a platform, where you can sit on a bench and look east toward the Hunters Point power plant and the East Bay hills.

- Turn right on the 400 block of Franconia. Several redwood-shingled houses dominate the street. Turn left to the (unmarked) Mayflower Stairway. Two palm trees have been planted at the beginning of the descent. Here you have a view of India Basin and Oakland.

- Continue down through the driveway to Holladay and turn left. The Bayshore Freeway (Hwy. 101) traffic noise is mitigated by double-paned windows and other insulation installed in the new and remodeled homes along the street. The slope is still undeveloped, but some live oaks have been planted.

- Turn left at Joy Stairway, where a corkscrew willow tree has been planted. I have fond memories of the first Joy Stairway—a few steps that led up to a pulpitlike structure, then continued in a haphazard

Joy Stairway

Adah Bakalinsky

fashion, up to Brewster. The slope was slippery and muddy then because of the heavy rains of 1982–83. The ambiance was rural, with gingham and calico accents. Almost 20 years later, the new pedestrian thoroughfares are built to conform to safety codes. But Nos. 16, 18, and 20 Joy are original flat-front Italianates from the 1870s and 1880s.

Will Kemp, the Shakespearean clown, jigged the 100 miles from London to Norwich on a bet, in February 1600.

▲ Continue up the wood steps to Brewster. Across from No. 138 Brewster, turn right onto Faith Stairway. This is a new concrete stairway that traverses a garden of sweet peas, poppies, lavender, ceanothus, coast live oaks, and pines. No. 159 Faith, built in 1901, features a stained-glass window. From here, the skywalk that arches over the Bayshore Freeway looks attractive.

◀ ▲ At the bottom of the stairs, turn left on Holladay and walk past Costa to Rutledge Stairway (next to No. 300 Holladay). It is an unmarked street right-of-way. You ascend the timber and metal stairway through a garden of redwoods, pines, a buckeye tree, and annuals. Walk up the new concrete stairs past the cul-de-sac of Mullen.

▲ To the right the city land is planted with trees. The left side of the stairway has some cottages. No. 43, built in 1895, is especially attractive in its siting among garden vines and trees on the lot. Continue to Brewster and turn left.

▲ No. 55 has an old-fashioned porch along the front of the house and some sculpture in the front garden. Walk past the retaining wall, then turn right, up the stairway to the entrance of Miller Memorial Grove/Dogpatch Garden. The stairway (left) goes up through the community garden. At the top, pass through the gate with the sign: THIS IS A NICE NEIGHBORHOOD GARDEN.

▲ You are now on Franconia, with Rutledge and Massasoit to the left. Go right on Franconia to descend the stairway to Montcalm. Left of the curved railroad-tie and pebble stairway are blackberry bushes. (Walk carefully on the short dirt stretch.) No. 109 Franconia is a Craftsman-style home that has an award-winning garden along Montcalm. Cross Montcalm and continue to Mullen. Turn left and ascend the stairway ramp. You pass a Japanese-style compound of several residences, built around a common courtyard.

▶ Follow the path to the crest of Peralta Point. City street rights-of-way and Open Space funding contributed to establishing this open area; it provides views of the downtown skyline from the Bechtel building to Twin Peaks. Plans for restoring native plants are still pending.

▶ Continue left on the pathway adjacent to the garden around the Point. Descend a short section of railroad-tie stairs, turn left, and left again to follow the path through an Open Space garden, created and maintained by neighbors at No. 300 Montcalm. (It won a San Francisco Beautiful award.)

▶ Cross Rutledge and ascend the Peralta Stairway. At the top you can see a San Francisco view that always makes me catch my breath. The house on your right has an unusual fan-shaped fence. Note the redwood tree at the corner of Samoset and Peralta. Continue on Peralta, past Ripley to your beginning.

Circling

BERNAL HEIGHTS WEST

Two Hills

A sunny neighborhood, Bernal Heights enjoys extraordinary views of the City. With the largest number of stairways of any neighborhood, it also has a greater variety of street names with historic associations than any other. Among them you find: Banks, Winslow, Putnam, Army, Moultrie, and Sumter that relate to the Civil War; Powhattan, Samoset, and Massasoit that relate to Native American leaders; and several that relate to the U.S. Colonial period. Bernal Heights has streets that change names, corners that don't coincide, some unpaved paths, and some of the most dedicated and active neighborhood-watch groups in the City. Neighbors here know how to work and cooperate with City agencies: they have been successful in establishing and preserving open space and community gardens wherever feasible.

▶ Begin your walk in an unusual circular configuration at Holly Park. Real estate developers gave it to the City in the 1860s hoping that an elite neighborhood would develop here, as it did in South Park. But the neighborhood became working class around 1900.

▶ Ascend the concrete stairway at Holly Park Circle from the north end of Bocana. Follow the circular path clockwise around the park. Rockrose, marguerites, salvia, and iris, and boxwood bushes have been planted along the slopes. Holly Hill (274') provides a view around the cardinal points of the compass. Behind you at the Bocana intersection is Bernal Heights Hill (325'), your destination. You can also see the dark, carnelian granite Bank of America building in the Financial District. Follow the walkway and near the Park St. intersection, you see the Bayview District and Hunters Point. Looking south from the Murray intersection you can see the blue water tower

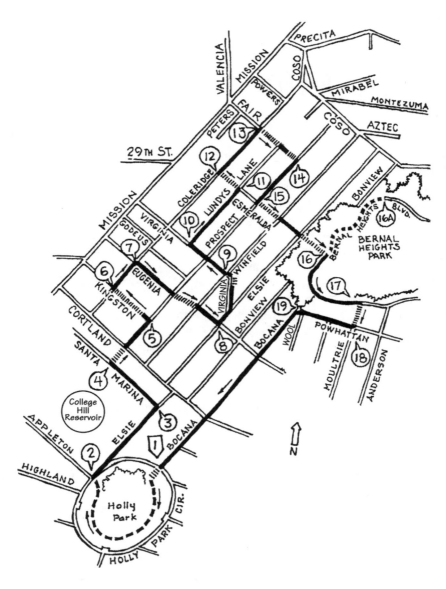

in McLaren Park. A grove of 30 olive trees, transplanted from the Civic Center in 1998, lines this eastern section of Holly Hill, as does a grove of eucalyptus. A magnolia tree memorial for Jonathan Hussey, who worked as a City planner, grows near the children's playground. Continue on the path that dips down to the Appleton intersection, from where you see the buildings of Diamond Heights.

▶ Turn right on Elsie. You pass the College Hill Reservoir, built in the mid 19th Century to bring water to the Mission District. Along the sidewalk you also pass Elsie Garden, the work of talented and caring neighbors. Turn left at Santa Marina, and turn right at the queen palm to descend the Prospect Stairway to Cortland. Walk through the Good Prospect Community Garden. It has a greater variety of plants than any other SLUG (San Francisco League of Urban Gardeners) garden: roses, sweet peas, thyme, lemon verbena, Russian sage, vegetables, and fruit trees. As you walk under the grape arbor, find a side path of tiled stepping-stones leading to a small, rustic bench.

WALK 20: Bernal Heights West Route

Public transportation: Muni Bus #24 (Divisadero) stops at Cortland and Bocana, about a block away.

1. Begin at Holly Park Circle and north side of Bocana.
2. Walk clockwise on circular path to Appleton and Elsie.
3. Right turn on Elsie to Santa Marina; turn left.
4. Right on Prospect Stwy. to Kingston.
5. Left on Kingston Stwy. to Coleridge.
6. Right on Coleridge to Eugenia.
7. Right on Eugenia St. and Stwy. to Elsie.
8. Left on Virginia to Winfield.
9. Follow Virginia Garden Walk to Lundys Lane.
10. Right on Lundys Lane to Esmeralda.
11. Left on Esmeralda Stwy.
12. Right on Coleridge to Fair.
13. Right on Fair Stwy. to Prospect.
14. Right on Prospect to Esmeralda.
15. Left on Esmeralda Stwy. to Bernal Heights Blvd.
16. Left on Bernal Heights Blvd. for views.
16a. Left to return on Blvd. to Moultrie.
17. Right on Moultrie Stwy. to Powhattan.
18. Right on Powhattan to Bocana.
19. Left on Bocana to your beginning.

- Continue on Prospect and turn left on Kingston. Follow the walkway to the concrete and steel stairway, built alongside the Franciscan Formation. You can see the non-identical twin spires of St. Paul's Church in Noe Valley, and above it Diamond Heights and Twin Peaks. Turn right on Coleridge to Eugenia. Walk up the angled Eugenia Stairway, indicated by bollards and a eucalyptus tree, flanked by agave and ivy, and shaded by gingko and pine trees. A sign announces EUGENIA GARDEN.

- At the top you cross Winfield, continue on Eugenia, and turn left on Elsie. The street divides, Virginia goes downhill and Elsie up. On the uphill side of the gore point, just past the ONE WAY sign, walk on the sidewalk to the left of No. 319, the shingled house with tile accents. Follow the Virginia Garden Walk, another neighborhood beautification project.

- Follow the left curve. Go past the first stairway to your left; descend the second stairway and cross Winfield. Continue down mostly elm tree-lined Virginia. No. 217 is a three-story Stick Italianate. Pass Prospect and turn right on Lundys Lane, one of my favorite streets. Carob trees planted along the street complement the cottages here.

- Turn left to descend the concrete Esmeralda Stairway, which is enhanced by plantings of ceanothus, sage, and daisies. At the bottom of the stairway is a viewing platform.

- Turn right on Coleridge. Note the Mini Park across the street. Continue to Fair; turn right and ascend the Fair Stairway. In 1990, a *Cinco de Mayo* dance was performed at the top of the stairway. The dancers were in costume and the music was live. (How about a coordinated dance performance taking place simultaneously on five stairways throughout the City? I've often imagined it!) Along the stairway you pass some neglected fenced-off gardens on either side. Continue past the brick-paved cul-de-sac of Lundys Lane.

- Turn right on Prospect, next to a garden with pines, eucalyptus, echium, pelargonium, and agapanthus. Continue over the hill past No. 34, one of the oldest homes in Bernal Heights. Situated on the original goat farm, the homestead has been extended from a simple, narrow clapboard with gables to a roomy, two-story, eight-room structure.

- Turn left onto another section of the Esmeralda Stairway—this one with steel handrails and lights, flowers along the edges, and rope swings hanging from the branches of tall trees. At the top of the stairway is the recently refurbished double slide. Adults like to try it, and they quickly arrive at the bottom. Several trees, including a large pepper, shade the picnic table and bench at the Winfield Plaza. Continue up the short street block of Esmeralda to the highest section of the stairway.

In 1885 Charles Lummis walked 3500 miles, from Cincinnati, Ohio, to Los Angeles in 143 days. He paid for his trip by writing articles about his adventures for the Los Angeles Times. *He fought off a wildcat, a mountain lion, escaped from convicts, and set his own arm. Subsequently he became City Editor of the* Los Angeles Times.

▶ This section of the Esmeralda Stairway leads through a shade garden of ferns and rhododendrons, another project of caring neighbors. A coast live oak is marked with a memorial plaque for the late Margaret Randolph, a Bernal Heights activist.

▶ At the top, surrounded by flowering plum and ceanothus, is the asphalt road that circles Bernal Heights Park. Neighbors succeeded 10 years ago in having the City close this section of road to cars, making it safe for walkers. Designated as a "natural area," the hill is where the Native Plant Society and the Bernal Hilltop Native Grassland Restoration Project have monthly work parties.

▶ The route around the hill is 1 mile long, and many people jog or walk its length. The view from here is one of the most rewarding in the City. Walk left as far as you like for the views, and then retrace your steps (south) to a west-facing bench where you can take in San Bruno Mountain, Twin Peaks, and Angel Island.

▶ Continue on the road as it curves left past the auto barrier. Then walk to the end of the chain-link fence and look for the beginning of the Moultrie Stairway, near the driveway of No. 123, (written on the fence) beside the multiple mailboxes. Bear right beside a wood fence and left under a eucalyptus. The little pebble path with wood waterstop steps becomes a concrete walk that goes past gardens. Walk on a ramp to Powhattan.

▶ Turn right and proceed along Powhattan to the end, past a cottage at the corner of Wool. The triangle-shaped garden across the street is a neighbor-initiated project.

▶ Turn left on Bocana to go downhill toward Holly Park and your beginning. When you cross Cortland, one of the major east-west streets and the major shopping street, you can bear left to an area of coffee houses and restaurants.

A Harmonious

McLAREN PARK & EXCELSIOR

Walk

John McLaren Park, located in the southeast corner of San Francisco, is the City's second largest park (318 acres) and one of its least known. In this walk you'll explore the seeps, ponds, and marshes of the park's well-tended northern edge. By traversing bridges and stairways you'll segue into the surrounding neighborhood, which still retains a relatively rustic ambiance. All these elements mingle harmoniously here.

The park was dedicated to John McLaren, who was the chief gardener of Golden Gate Park for 60 years. While land purchases for the park began in the late 1920s, its designated area was not fully acquired until the 1970s, due to short funding and dozens of farming inholdings. In 1987 a bond issue providing 2.4 million dollars to implement the Master Plan for McLaren Park was passed. It provided for a felicitous park design, with cypress and redwood groves, cattail marshes, and riparian areas where willow and horsetail grow.

> *"I love walking in London," said Mrs. Dalloway.*
> *"Really it's better than walking in the country."*
> —from *Mrs. Dalloway* by Virginia Woolf

▶ Begin in the 300 block of Gambier at Felton and walk toward Burrows. The attached houses on your left (east) date from the 1940s and 1950s, but on the right are cottages of the early 1900s. These occupy two or three lots with room for extensive yards and outbuildings. Gravel driveways and well-tended gardens lend them a rural touch.

▶ Enter McLaren Park from Burrows and Gambier. A neighbor enjoying the view from his garage told me the park across the street was just rough pasture when he moved here in 1961; he still feels as if he lives in the country.

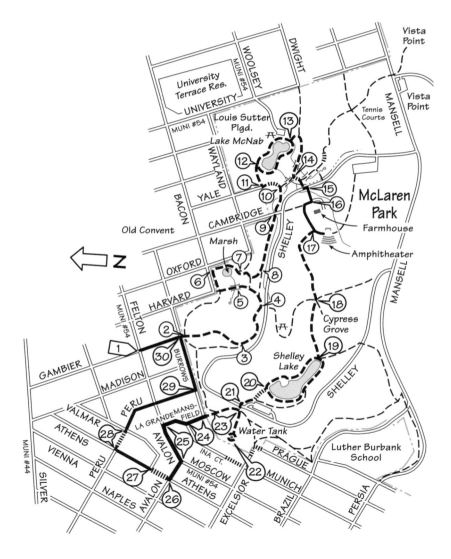

Walk 21: McLaren Park & Excelsior Route

Public Transportation: Muni Bus #54.

1. Begin in 300 block of Gambier at Felton. Walk to Burrows.
2. Cross Burrows into Park. Continue straight on descending path.
3. Follow curve of trail along eucalyptus grove and shortly after, a redwood grove.
4. Continue left from sandbox.
5. Cross a concrete bridge.
6. Continue around left edge of marsh on asphalt path.
7. Turn right at basketball court.
8. Turn left to go along path beside Shelley Dr.
9. Cross Cambridge and continue on path; bear left at next junction.
10. Descend Stwy. to Yale.
11. Turn right. Descend driveway to Lake McNab.
12. Walk either way around Lake McNab.
13. Leave lake via sandy playground. Bear right on paved path.
14. After the footbridge, take left path and railroad tie Stwy.; then bear right on side path to Shelley Dr.
15. Cross Shelley Dr. Walk up paved driveway opposite.
16. Turn right, then left (around farmhouse).
17. Bear right to go up the path from the amphitheater.
18. At path and trail intersection, go straight ahead; continue ahead at the cypress grove junction on the level path.
19. At south tip of Shelley Lake, walk either way around the lake.
20. At north end turn left. Climb long railroad-tie Stwy. to hill crest.
21. Continue past parking lot to Shelley Dr.; cross it and ascend long paved driveway.
22. Circle counterclockwise around water tower.
23. Retrace steps to Shelley Dr. Turn left on paved path. Stay left at playground.
24. Exit park at corner of Burrows and Mansfield. Continue straight on Mansfield, which turns into La Grande, for one block.
25. Left on Avalon. Continue on Avalon one block to Moscow, and right for one block more to Athens.
26. Turn right; ascend Athens Stwy.
27. Continue on Athens for one block to Peru.
28. Ascend Peru Stwy. to Valmar. Continue on Peru for two blocks to Burrows.
29. Turn left on Burrows to Gambier.
30. Turn left to return to 300 block of Gambier.

Excelsior

- Proceed straight on an asphalt walkway that soon begins to descend around the top of a large grassy bowl. Along the trail are eucalyptus and Monterey pine groves (remnants of farm-era wood lots). Follow the curve of the trail along the redwood grove and by a young live oak. Keep left along the path parallel to Shelley Dr. You glimpse the Portola and Bayview neighborhoods and the East Bay Hills.

- Where the path meets wide Shelley Drive, there's a round sandbox in the middle. Across the street (right) is a large group-picnic area. Proceed left from the sandbox, keeping left along the path.

- The path enters a grove of alder and redwood and crosses a concrete bridge. The creek below flows from a natural spring, just ahead to your left. Look for the unmowed grass and horsetails (equisetum). To see where it flows, turn right at the corner of Harvard and Bacon, walk for one block, and turn right again. On your right is a tiny pond filled with cattails. The water's surface is nearly covered with a floating carpet of duckweed. Though human-made, the pond is home to raccoons and small birds. It captures runoff from the grassy bowl you descended from Gambier Street and keeps the adjacent neighborhood dry.

- Looking left across Oxford Street you can see a large, rustic green-house, a remnant of the Portola neighborhood's agricultural heritage, now squeezed between newer houses.

- Continue around the left edge of the marsh on the asphalt path. Beyond the round, recently refurbished restroom, turn right at the basketball court and clamber up a steep path to some large cypress trees.

- Now turn left and saunter along the path beside Shelley Drive, enjoying the broad views. Behind you is the pond; to your left is the Portola District. The tall, Italian-style tower is Bridgemont Academy, a private school occupying an old convent. To the east you can see the flat expanse of the University Mound reservoirs, and get a glimpse of San Francisco Bay and the East Bay Hills.

- At the intersection of Shelley Dr. and Cambridge, cross Cambridge and descend a winding asphalt path through a dense pine grove. Bear left at the next two junctions. Railroad-tie steps descend to the tip of Yale. Turn right and descend the paved driveway to Lake McNab, a human-made lake fed by natural springs and runoff from the north slope of McLaren Park. Two big cattail "islands" provide cover for many kinds of birds, including egrets, herons, ducks, and coots. Neighbors enjoy the stroll around the paved lakeshore.

▲ Walk either way around the lake to the far (south) end, where you find a wood-topped drain cover, swings, and a small sandbox; picnic tables provide a pleasant place to sit. Leaving the lake via the sandbox playground, you ascend (right) on a paved path leading past a thicket of willow and alder. Just beyond the first zigzag footbridge, take the left path with railroad-tie steps. Bear right on the short side path to wide Shelley Drive.

▲ Cross Shelley carefully and walk up the paved driveway opposite, signed for JOHN MCLAREN AMPHITHEATER. About 100 feet up the driveway take the right fork. Turn left at the first opening and follow the PARKING sign through the small lot for the handicapped. Ahead (left) is the stunning, recently renovated amphitheater. With the increasing numbers of musical performances recently held here, this facility may soon soon get the use that it deserves.

▲ Follow the gravel path that starts at the parking lot gate, climbing to the left through open grassland. Red-tailed hawks sometimes perch on the trees on the right of the path. At a cypress grove near the top of the hill is a complex intersection of paths and trails. Continue straight ahead on the level path crossing a grassy slope edged with coyote brush. In the spring native wildflowers are abundant (look but don't pick!). Below (right) is the group picnic area you saw near the beginning of the walk.

▲ Your path leads to the south tip of Shelley Lake, a reservoir for the park's irrigation water. This lake is windier and more exposed than other sections of the park. A chain-link fence incompletely separates the lake (several openings let you get close to the water) from the rocky shoreline. Walk along either shore. At the north end, turn left and climb a long railroad-tie stairway to the hill crest.

▲ Continue past the parking lot to Shelley Dr. On the hilltop ahead is the blue Excelsior water tower, a neighborhood landmark. Cross Shelley Dr. and ascend the long paved driveway. Circle counterclockwise around the water tower to enjoy the panoramic view, one of the grandest in the City. To the north are Bernal Heights, Diamond Heights, Glen Canyon, and Twin Peaks, plus a bit of downtown skyline. To the west is City College, and to the south is the Excelsior District and San Bruno Mountain.

- After savoring the view, retrace your steps toward Shelley Dr. and turn left on the paved path. Stay left at the playground and exit the park at the corner of Burrows and Mansfield. Take a look at No. 73 Mansfield, a charming little country house surrounded by trees.

- Walk ahead one block on Mansfield, and then bear right on La Grande to Avalon. The church on the corner was formerly a neighborhood grocery store. (Muni Bus #54 bus stops here.) Turn left on Avalon and follow it (as it curves right) to Athens. Turn right and ascend the concrete Athens Stairway. City College gradually comes into view. Continue on Athens for one block to Peru. Your view ahead is toward the northeast.

- Ascend Peru Stairway. The adjoining hillside was a dumping ground and an eyesore in the 1970s until a grassroots group, the Hilltop Block Club, banded together. In cooperation with the Recreation and Park Department and the City's Open Space committee, the Club retained landscape architect Richard Schadt to design the hillside garden and stairway. Seventy neighborhood residents cooperated in digging, planting, and watering more than 150 trees and shrubs, which had been propagated at the Golden Gate Park nursery. The basic work was completed in 1982.

- The serpentine stairway is built of aggregate and railroad ties. Trees on the slopes are Australian willow, *Myoporum*, Italian pine, and flowering plum. The view behind you includes Mount Davidson (with the cross) and Glen Canyon Park.

- You enter an open grassy knoll at the top, Valmar Terrace (a perfect place to sit and read or simply gaze around). The neighbor on the left tends the area, watering, picking up garbage, and planting flowers on her adjoining lot, so that everyone can enjoy the greenery.

- Continue on Peru. (The view now takes in San Francisco General Hospital, the shipyards, Mt. Diablo across the Bay and, to the left, Roundtop Peak.) No. 747 Peru is below street level. Above the number is a little Buddha, lemon trees grow in the yard, and a penthouse has been built facing east. To the right you see again the blue water tower in McLaren Park, and as you continue walking on Peru, you face the Park.

- At Peru and Burrows the uneven macadam and adjoining McLaren Park can make you feel like you've been out for a country walk. Turn left on Burrows to reach Gambier and your beginning.

Follow the Curve,

FAIRMOUNT HEIGHTS, DIAMOND HEIGHTS, & (a bit of) GLEN CANYON

Follow the View

The Diamond Heights neighborhood was built on 325 acres of craggy, hilly terrain after World War II, when federal redevelopment money became available for construction. A range of modest-to-luxurious homes, townhouses, apartments, and condominiums were built, trees were planted, and stairways were constructed. Diamond Heights is bounded by important corridor streets, O'Shaughnessy Blvd., Portola Dr., Clipper St., and Diamond Heights Blvd.; and by the 300-foot-deep Glen Canyon, which separates it from Miraloma to the west and Glen Park to the east.

▶ Beginning at the shopping-center corner of Diamond Heights Blvd. (No. 5290) and Gold Mine Dr., walk south on Diamond Heights Blvd. At the next intersection, turn left on Diamond St. and follow the curve to Beacon St. I love to take visitors here for the remarkable vista we get, walking along the ridge of Beacon on the new footpath. Because people love shortcuts, cycle tracks and walking tracks crisscross down the slope, which is part of the Open Space program.

▶ The Harry Stairway begins between Nos. 190 and 200 Beacon. It is very easy to miss because it looks like a private walkway. The stairway is constructed of both wood and concrete. You descend parallel to numerous conifers growing in the lot on the right. Monterey cypress branches overhang the stairway. I like the surprising contrast in atmosphere and vegetation between an urban street and a forest path. The long Harry Stairway lets you see the variety in homes alongside, which establishes an individual style to the vicinity.

- When you're parallel to the banana trees, views—Yerba Buena Island and the Bay Bridge to the east, and the spires of St. Paul's Church and downtown San Francisco north—become visible. All the while, nearest you, African daisies, ivy, geraniums, wild onion, pittisporum, yucca, lily of the Nile, datura, abutilon, nasturiums, and hydrangeas provide a celebration of color and foliage.

- The Harry Stairway ends at LAIDLEY 100. You are now in the Fairmount Heights neighborhood that was platted in 1864. The boundaries are Castro to the west, Arlington to the east, 30th to the north, and Bemis to the south. Cobb and Sinton were the real estate developers. Old photos show vernacular cottages along unpaved paths and pine groves.

- Turn right on Laidley. A short street (one of my favorites), it is, essentially, a street of cottages. A resident of the street, architect Jeremy Kotas has been responsible for the dramatic metamorphosis from simple cottages to imaginative, contemporary dwellings. You pass several homes he worked on: Nos. 102, 128, 134, 123, 140, and 135. No. 140 is known in the neighborhood as the Owl House because of the "eyebrows," and No.134 as the Sand Castle because of the undulating first story.

- The palatial three-story, Second Empire and Italianate home, No. 192–194 (near Fairmount), now an apartment house, was built in 1872. It is commonly known as the Bell Mystery House. The death of the owner, Thomas Bell, a San Francisco financier, occurred under mysterious circumstances. His wife, Teresa, and his housekeeper, Mary Ann Pleasant, may have possibly been involved. Without a satisfactory explanation, it has been fodder for a neighborhood myth. Actually the interesting character is Pleasant, known as Mammy Pleasant, a free-born black woman from Philadelphia. She was a celebrated cook who worked for wealthy families, a dedicated Abolitionist, and an entrepreneur. She owned laundries, boardinghouses, and brothels. (See *Mammy Pleasant* and *Mammy Pleasant's Partner* by Helen Holdredge and *A Cast of Hawks* by Milton Gould.)

A walk should have simplicity and complexity,
contrast and unity.

—A. Packerman

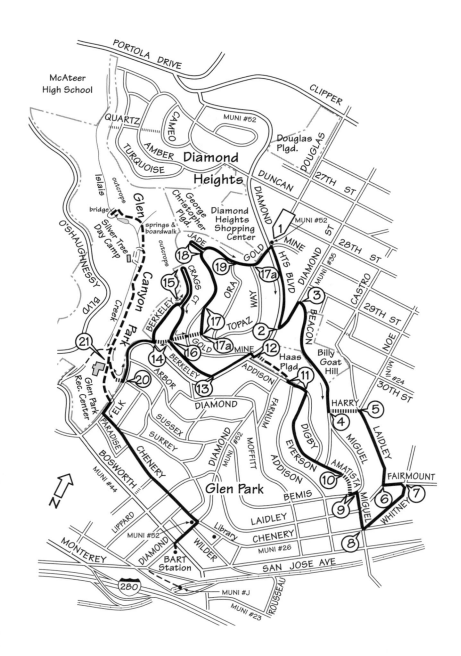

Turn left on Fairmount. No. 226 is a tuck-in, set deep into the lot where residents can enjoy an enviable view. Make a right turn on Whitney, a small street with several row Queen Annes. Turn right to Chenery, the Glen Park neighborhood shopping street. Farther along

WALK 22: Fairmount Heights, Diamond Heights, & (a bit of) Glen Canyon Route

Public Transportation: Muni Bus #52 stops at Diamond Heights Blvd. and Gold Mine.

1. From Diamond Heights Blvd. shopping center (No. 5290) and Gold Mine Dr., walk south on Diamond Heights Blvd. to Diamond St.
2. Left on Diamond St. to Beacon.
3. Right on Beacon to Harry Stwy., next to No. 190 Beacon.
4. Descend Stwy. to Laidley.
5. Right on Laidley.
6. Left on Fairmount.
7. Right on Whitney.
8. Right to Chenery, and right again on Miguel.
9. Left on Bemis, and then right to ascend Amatista Stwy.
10. Continue to Everson bearing left.
11. Continue straight ahead on Addison to Diamond Heights Blvd.
12. Cross the Blvd. Left on Diamond Heights Blvd. to Berkeley Way.
13. Right on Berkeley Way.
14. Next to No. 99, left to descend Onique Stwy. Right on Berkeley Way to see rock formation near corner of Crags Ct.
15. Go to end of Crags Ct. Return and continue across on Berkeley Way.
16. Next to No. 100 Berkeley Way, ascend Stwy. (left) to Gold Mine (No. 400). Continue up Onique Stwy. to Topaz (No. 243).
17. Left on Topaz. Right on Gold Mine Dr.
17a. *(optional) Right on Topaz. Right on Gold Mine Dr. to your beginning.*
18. Walk into Jade Pl. for view.
19. Continue on Gold Mine to Diamond Heights Blvd to your beginning.
20. *(optional) If you'd like to walk on the open path in Glen Park Canyon, continue south on Diamond Heights Blvd. to Elk. At Sussex, turn right into the Canyon by descending the stairway. Walk on road, cross bridge, walk to the end and return.*
21. *Continue south on Elk , left on Chenery, the "downtown" Glen Park. Visit the storefront Glen Park Library at No. 653 Chenery. The Muni Bus #52 crosses Chenery at Diamond.*

Harry Street

the street a coffee house, a bakery, the hardware store, and the friendly storefront branch library convey the essence of a small town Main Street. (A new library is in the planning stage.)

- Turn right at Miguel and walk uphill to Bemis. Turn left and ascend the Amatista Stairway to Everson. A shopping center was proposed for the triangle near the top of the stairs, but residents opposed it, and the area is now a small park.

- Everson is one of the oldest sections of the Diamond Heights Redevelopment Area. A resident told me that her home and the house at No. 50 Everson, which was made with lumber from the 1939 Golden Gate International Exposition on Treasure Island, were the only two structures on the street in 1957.

- Continue on the left side of Everson for the view: Bayview Heights, the blue water tower of the Excelsior neighborhood, and San Bruno Mtn. with its radio towers. Where Everson ends at Digby, turn left, pass the fire station, and walk through the basketball court of the 4-plus acre Walter Haas Park and Playground, an inviting place for picnicking, playing, and just sitting.

- Walk up the short railroad-tie stairway to Diamond Heights Blvd. If you'd like to return to the beginning of the walk at this point, turn right. If you'd like to continue on the Diamond Heights portion of the walk, cross the Blvd. and turn left. You pass GOLD MINE 000.

- At Berkeley Way turn right. Next to No. 99, descend Onique Stairway to the lower loop of Berkeley Way. You are looking down on Glen Canyon Park, where, in the 1800s, carnivals, parades, picnics, dances, and other amusements took place. Continue to the right to see the extraordinary rock formation near the corner of Crags Ct. One of the first residents on Crags Ct. bought a house here to practice rock climbing.

- Continue right around Crags Ct. into Berkeley Way. Eucalyptus and pine have been planted here and in the hills (right) above O'Shaughnessy Blvd. Next to No. 100 Berkeley Way ascend Onique Stairway. Midway you're next to No. 400 Gold Mine. Cross the street and continue upward. At the top we are next to No. 243 Topaz.

- Turn left (but see below) on Topaz and right on Gold Mine Dr. (679'). Walk into Jade Place (left) for mini views of the Bay Bridge and skyscrapers between the houses and garages. Continue around to your left, walking downhill on Gold Mine Dr. to the beginning.

▶ An alternate route, which I like very much, is to turn right on Topaz. As you walk along the ridge near No. 131, an extraordinary view unfolds before you—east and south. Continue down the hill to Gold Mine; bear right to your beginning.

Further Ambling

While restoration is in progress in Glen Canyon, you cannot walk along the left side of Islais Creek. However, by walking on the main road (the right side), you can see the plants that grow so well near and in water—willows, sedges, and equisetum. You can see the native wildflowers growing on the slopes of the hill. You pass the nursery school that is on the left side of the creek, and walk over two boardwalks. A log fence is now on your left. By walking across the wood bridge, you can see the many birds, the walkers and their dogs, and enjoy at close range the 300-foot canyon in the middle of the City, which exposes the massive Franciscan Formation.

Now You See It,

Now You Don't:

Discover the Fog

& Light

of San Francisco

At 938 feet elevation, Mt. Davidson is the highest hill in San Francisco. Known in the 1850s as Blue Mountain, it was renamed Mt. Davidson in 1911 to honor George Davidson (1825–1911), first surveyor of the mountain, internationally renown scientist, and president of the California Academy of Sciences. Mt. Davidson was dedicated as a city park in December 1929.

The idea of a cross on Mt. Davidson originated with James Decatur, and the first Easter service was held in 1923. Ten years later President Franklin Roosevelt lit the cross via telegraph. The City annually illuminated it during Christmas and Easter seasons, and thousands of people have attended the Easter Sunday sunrise services. In 1996, the

U.S. Appeals Court ruled that the religious symbol violates the Constitutional separation of church and state.

In 1997, San Francisco approved the sale of the cross and surrounding one-third acre to the Armenian American Organization of Northern California for $26,000. It is to be preserved as a historic landmark in memory of the 1,500,000 Armenian victims of genocide perpetrated by the Turkish government from 1915 to 1918.

With slopes covered with pine and eucalyptus, walking the trails can be confusing because the Department of Recreation and Parks has not yet put up signage. My problem was to find the trail leading to the

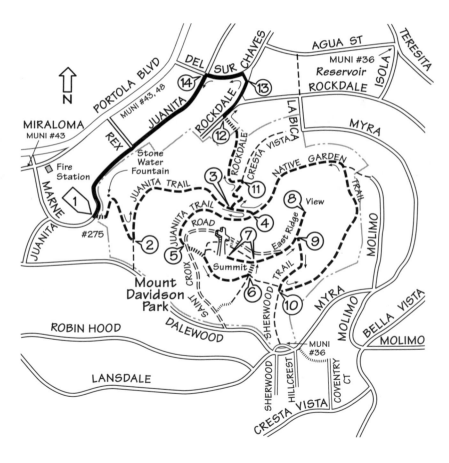

desired exit. Though I tried the walk at different times with various friends, the problem continued. An engineer friend finally solved it by advising, "Keep it simple." It worked. We found two beautiful stone stairways, the breathtaking view, trails with blackberries (edible) and Coast strawberries (inedible), ferns, and wildflowers—forget-me-nots, nasturtiums, and monkey flowers. Breathing ocean air and eucalyptus, we were in the City but also quite removed from it.

While historic trail names are extant from 1935, when the WPA trail-blazed Mt. Davidson, without signage I've resorted to two non-historic names. Sherwood Trail is named for the street at the end of the

WALK 23: Mt. Davidson Route

Public Transportation: Muni Bus #43 (Masonic) stops at Miraloma and Marne.

1. Follow Marne from Miraloma to your beginning at #275 Juanita. Beside it is a stone stairway that you ascend.
2. Turn left on Juanita Trail.
3. Where Cresta Vista and Rockdale trails join your route on the left, continue up toward the right.
4. At junction (ahead) with Native Garden Trail, switchback right, staying on the Juanita Trail.
5. Cross the access (St. Croix) road, and ascend a stone Stwy. and path bearing left.
6. Ascend a stone Stwy.
7. Now at the summit, the cross is to your left. (Retrace your steps to exit on Juanita Dr., or continue as decribed below.)
8. Follow the East Ridge Trail to the panoramic look-out.
9. Retrace your steps from the viewpoint to the first left; take it to descend a medium-steep gravel road south (the Sherwood Trail).
10. At the next junction bear left on the Native Garden Trail, which descends and partly circumnavigates the peak. Where it eventually joins the Juanita Trail at the switchback (see 4), turn right to descend. At the next junction, turn right down the Cresta Vista Trail. It switchbacks a couple times before reaching the junction with the Rockdale Trail.
11. Take the Rockdale Trail (left) down to a stone Stwy., and descend it to Rockdale St.
12. Turn right on Rockdale.
13. Veer left on Chaves to Del Sur.
14. Turn left to Juanita and your beginning.

trail. The Native Garden Trail was always a footpath and not included in the original park.

- Begin west of Mt. Davidson, at the stone stairway next to No. 275 Juanita. Your route is *up*. Blackberries growing along the stairway are delicious in season. When you reach a non-functioning drinking fountain—a useful landmark—ascend toward the right. Then, climb toward the left. Wildflowers grow alongside. At the next fork with the Cresta Vista Trail, ascend to the right. Where the the Native Garden Trail joins your trail at the point of a switchback, turn sharply right to continue up the Juanita Trail.

- Near the top is the Saint Croix Rd. (for vehicles). Continue on the ascending path and stairway. Turn left on the stone stairway to the top, near the cross. Look right to see the view. *If you'd like to retrace the route down, begin your descent on the stone stairway. At the bottom of the stairway, turn right, cross the road, and continue down. Exit as you began, next to No. 275 Juanita.*

- To circumnagivate the summit and loop back to your beginning at No. 275 Juanita, from the summit follow the East Ridge Trail to the panoramic look-out, then partly retrace your steps to descend along the first left-branching road, the Sherwood Trail.

- Soon after the Sherwood Trail enters the woods, bear left on the Native Garden Trail. It descends and partly circumnavigates the peak, overlooking here the Miraloma Park neighborhood. It eventually rejoins the Juanita Trail at the switchback.

- When you meet the Juanita Trail in the woods, turn right to descend it. When you shortly reach another junction, turn right down the Cresta Vista Trail. It switchbacks a couple times before reaching the junction (left) with the Rockdale Trail.

Jamaicans don't say, "Goodbye." They say, "Walk good."

- Take the Rockdale Trail down to a stone stairway, and descend it to Rockdale St. Turn right on Rockdale. Veer left on Chaves to Del Sur. Turn left to Juanita and your beginning. On the way you pass Franciscan Formation outcrops at the Park's edge, and some seeps (active in winter) that encourage ferns, eucalyptus, and other lush vegetation.

Further Ambling

To traverse Mt. Davidson and exit by another trailhead, from the summit follow the East Ridge Trail to the panoramic look-out, partly retrace your steps to descend along the first left-branching road, the Sherwood Trail. Keep going ahead where the Native Garden Trail branches left. You can descend the Sherwood Trail down to Myra and Sherwood Streets, where you can take Muni Bus #36 to Forest Hill Station or Balboa Park Bart.

You could also walk left on Myra around the Park on the city streets to La Bica. Turn right on La Bica, walk one block to Rockdale, turn left for a block, and then continue, as decribed above, to your beginning at No. 275 Juanita.

Mt. Davidson is part of the enormous area west of Twin Peaks, and is surrounded by sub-neighborhood sections: Sherwood Forest (there's a Robin Hood Dr. here), Westwood Highlands, and Miraloma Park. Larger homes can be found west and north of Mt. Davidson, the smaller ones in the eastern Miraloma section. Feel free to ramble through the various surrounding neighborhoods. You will see magnificent views beside Miraloma School at Omar and Myra Streets, and from Marietta Dr. and Bella Vista.

An Informal

Bibliography

Among favorite books that I keep on shelves at eye-level for easy access, I have Doris Muscatine's *Old San Francisco: The Biography of a City From Early Days to the Earthquake* (New York, NY: G.P. Putnam's Sons, 1975). I enjoy her writing as well as her scholarship. I recommend it without reservation.

Also on my shelves is David Myrick's now out-of-print, *San Francisco's Telegraph Hill* (Berkeley, CA: Howell-North Books, 1972). It's a priceless history with archival photographs.

Trustworthy reference books to have at hand are: Gladys Hansen's *San Francisco Almanac* (San Francisco, CA: Chronicle Books, 1995), and Judith Lynch Waldhorn and Sally Woodbridge's *Victoria's Legacy, Tours of San Francisco Bay Area Architecture* (San Francisco, CA: 101 Productions, 1978).

Randolph Delehanty's *Walks and Tours in the Golden Gate City* (San Francisco, The Dial Press, 1980) is an enlightening, opinionated commentary on the architecture throughout the City.

List of Stairways

While this is not a complete listing of stairways in San Francisco, I've tried to list the ones in neighborhoods that are part of routes used by residents. I've updated the list of neighborhood stairways, adding the new ones built during the past three years. While some have no nameplates, they are all listed in the Thomas maps.

No single factor can sum up the character of a stairway. It may be 100 steps but easy (Diamond and 22nd St.), or 30 steps and difficult (Collingwood St.). There are charming stairways (Pemberton) or utilitarian stairways (Stonestown). We have elegant concrete stairways (Alta Plaza Park) and we have wood stairways (Joy). We have stairways bordered by trees, shrubs, flowers, stones, broken glass, railings, Victorian houses, and lean-tos.

Stairways are difficult to push into categories—it seems easier to classify neighborhoods than stairways. Forest Hill and Forest Knolls are unusual in settings and stairways. Golden Gate Heights and Noe Valley have well-designed networks of stairways and retaining walls. Diamond Heights has a series of very long stairways. Telegraph Hill and Russian Hill have alleys and stairways and many houses that have no street access. Living along the Filbert and Greenwich stairways in the Telegraph Hill area is an incentive to purchase lightweight furniture, like futons.

Russian Hill, surrounded by other hill neighborhoods, gives a feeling of greater separation with its cul-de-sacs within cul-de-sacs (Vallejo and Florence). Upper Market is an unusual conglomerate of leveled, fenced-off, or permanently closed-off stairways. The "unbuildable" formerly empty lots in Bernal Heights and Twin Peaks have become sites for well-designed domiciles. East Bernal Heights is undergoing significant, dramatic changes.

Above all, this is a participatory book. The fun is in the walking, in discovering your own variations, in conversations struck up along the way, and in exhilarating views of this extraordinary City.

Ratings

My stairway ratings are based on what struck me most during a walk: steepness, length, location, elevation, or beauty—and any combination of these attributes.

5 The Scheherazade category. These stairways surprise the walker. They may be elegant or rustic; they may be short or long. They exhibit variety, stir the imagination, and delight the senses.

4 Impressive qualities with minor shortcomings; one outstanding aspect, or extremely attractive section.

3 Little known but deserve wider recognition because of the environs, man-made or natural. Neighborhood is generally very attractive.

2 Intrinsic to neighborhood history and ambiance. Well-trodden. In most cases, the architectural context rates considerably higher than the stairway itself, or the view may be worth the visit. It's a pretty straightforward stairway of no great beauty.

1 It may be so boring that you'll fall asleep on the first landing.

* A * stair might be well worth visiting if it were located in a safe neighborhood. This stairway is only for the knowledgeable resident, the wary aficionado.

/ The symbol / stands for the word "between."

ANZA VISTA

A neighborhood surrounding the University of San Francisco complex. Small well-kept homes from the 1950s and the Victorian era are part of this area.

2 Arbol Lane/Barcelona & Encanto & Turk. Next to No. 125 Anza Vista. *Good everyday route.*

2 Arguello/Anza & Edward into Rossi Recreation Center. *Large granite planter bowls at entrance of two granite stairways.*

2 Dicha Alley/Lupine & Wood. *Useful and used.*

2 Ewing at Nos. 196–200, to Anza near Collins. *Ewing Court was a baseball field at one time. Clever.*

4 Lone Mountain from 401 Parker to Beaumont to Stanyan to Rossi. *Long twitton, trees, church spires, views of Angel Island and west; nice series of Victorians on McAllister off Parker.*

BALBOA PARK

Indian street names abound in this neighborhood. Also has underground waterways, a creek and the old Cayuga Lake.

2   Balboa Park/San Jose Ave., near Ocean.
2   Balbao Park Bart Station.
2   Cayuga/Naglee & Alemany.
2   Oneida/Alemany & Cayuga. *Practical.*
1   Restani/Cayuga & Alemany. Next to No. 718 Geneva. *Practical. Only residents know it.*
2   Rousseau/Alemany & Mission.

BAYVIEW

Some historic buildings in this neighborhood.

*   Bayview Park. *All concrete.*
*   Gilroy Street/Jamestown.
*   Hawes & Innes.
*   Innes (next to Mt. Spring).
*   LaSalle/Mendall & Lane.
*   LaSalle & Osceola to Health Center.
*   Mini Park, at Lillian & Beatrice.
*   Quesada/Newhall & 3rd Street.
*   Thornton/3rd Street & Latona.

BERNAL HEIGHTS

A neighborhood mix of professionals, blue-collar workers, and artists. Most stairways have adjoining gardens; new stairways are in the planning stage.

1   Appleton/San Jose Ave. & Mission. *Utilitarian.*
2   Aztec/Shotwell & Stoneman. *Stoneman was a Union general in the Civil War.*
3   Bessie /up to Shotwell and Mirabel. *Narrow, unexpected. Half-size lots on Bessie.*
4   Brewster Stairway & Footpath/Rutledge, Costa & Mullen. Next to No. 115 Rutledge. *New, concrete up to "Dogpatch" Garden. Wood stairs up through poplars.*

2 Chapman & Bernal Heights Blvd. *Concrete. Native shrubs on slopes.*

2 Cortland/Prospect & Santa Marina

2 Coso Avenue/Prospect & Winfield. *View; cars from private driveway have to cross the stairs.*

4 Esmeralda/Winfield to Prospect to Lundys Lane to Coleridge.

3 Esmeralda/Brewster & Franconia. *Renovated. Elevated above landscaped hillside. Timber and concrete; benches and lighting. Views.*

4 Eugenia/Prospect & Winfield. *Among trees.*

1 Eve Stairway/upper & lower Holladay/Wright & Peralta. *A wraith of itself.*

2 Coleridge & Prospect. *Grove of trees at top. Gardens need work. View.*

2 Faith Stairway/Bayshore & Holladay. *Part of a pedestrian overpass; an opportunity to hear increases in decibels from auto traffic.*

3 Faith/Brewster & Holladay. *New access.*

4 Franconia/Brewster at Costa & Franconia. *Community garden, 1991. Railroad-tie stwy., trees, view toward Bay & Hunters Point.*

3 Franconia/Mullen & Montcalm. *Wooden, short. Shrubbery and trees alongside. View.*

3 Franconia/Mullen & Peralta & Montcalm. *Concrete, wood, landscaped.*

3 Franconia/Montcalm & Rutledge. *Wood & railroad-tie beside No. 199 Montcalm.*

3 Harrison/Ripley & Norwich. *Wood and concrete stwy., benches, lighting. Great view of downtown. Egger Open Space garden. Builder/subdivider put in stairway.*

1 Holladay/Peralta & Adam.

4 Holladay/Peralta & Bayshore. *View the link between an isolated, urban neighborhood and the main traffic arteries north and south.*

2 Holly Park/Bocana.

2 Holly Park/Highland.

2 Holly Park/Murray.

2 Holly Park/Park. Across from Junipero Serra School.

5 Joy/Holladay & Brewster. *Rural. New wood stairway and benches. Existing gardens to be preserved.*

3 Kingston/Coleridge & Prospect. *Semblance of floating stairs. Railing. Long footpath and rock formation alongside.*

3 Mayflower/Holladay & Franconia. *New access, wood stairway, trees— maytens, oak, purple leaf plum.*

1 Mayflower/Bradford & Carver. *Railroad-tie, short.*

5 Mirabel/at No. 11, to Precita. *Hidden. Extremely narrow.*

2 Montcalm/Wright & Peralta. *Rustic; through garden.*

3   Moultrie/Bernal Heights Blvd. & Powhattan. *Concrete plus footpath. Truly hidden and rural. Plantings alongside. First decisive victory of the Revolution was at Ft. Moultrie, SC, in 1776.*

3   Mullen/Franconia. *Mullen is a fanciful landlocked street in some spots. Enter at sign,* THIS IS A NICE NEIGHBORHOOD GARDEN.

2   Mullen, next to No. 146. *Concrete. Goes to next level.*

4   Nevada St. *Community Gardens.*

4   Peralta/Samoset & Mullen. *Magnificent gardens, extraordinary views.*

1   Richland/Mission & San Jose.

3   Rosenkranz/Chapman & Powhattan. *Rural, view, hillside plantings. Concrete with railing.*

4   Rutledge/Holladay, Mullen, Brewster, Peralta & Wolf Patch Community Garden. *Pedestrian path. Renovated; wide neighborhood use.*

3   Shotwell/Mirabel & Bessie. *Hidden—you wouldn't think to look for it. 1906 earthquake cottages on Shotwell. 12 ½-foot-wide lots on Bessie.*

3   Tompkins/Putnam & Nevada. *Stairway in much better condition than nearby fence. New tree plantings. View of industrial side of the city.*

3   Virginia/Eugenia & Winfield. *Part of a stairway series from retaining wall to lower level.*

BUENA VISTA

An old neighborhood with large mansions and converted flats.

3   Alpine/Wailer & Duboce. *Sidewalk stairway.*

3   Ashbury Terrace/at No. 64, near Piedmont.

4   Baker & Haight at Buena Vista East into Buena Vista Park.

2   Buena Vista East/No. 437, into Buena Vista Park. *Wooden. One of a series of three.*

4   Buena Vista Terrace/Buena Vista East & Duboce into Buena Vista Park. *Ornament above entrance wall gives unusual effect. Curving steps. View.*

*   Buena Vista West/Haight, into Buena Vista Park. *Lovely. One of the early, beautiful San Francisco neighborhoods—but be careful in your wanderings.*

4   Buena Vista West & Java/into Buena Vista Park. *Wooden.*

*   Central & Buena Vista West/into Buena Vista Park. *Stone stairway.*

4   Corona Heights Park. *New series of wooden stairs, new plantings by Native Plant Society. Surrounds Randall Junior Museum.*

3   DeForest/Beaver & Flint. *A stairway street, 3 feet wide and 125 feet long, built around 1975. At the top is Corona Heights Park.*

3   Duboce/Castro & Alpine. *Special. 25% grade.*

3   Frederick & Buena Vista West/into Buena Vista Park. *Concrete, wide. Should be extended.*

4   Welland Lathrop Memorial Walk/into Buena Vista Park. Across from 547 Buena Vista West. *Pine trees, view. Lathrop was one of the early modern dance teachers in San Francisco.*

2   Lyon & Haight/into Buena Vista Park.

2   Park Hill & Buena Vista East/into Buena Vista Park. *New stairways are being built in Buena Vista Park.*

4   Waller/Broderick & Buena Vista West. *Sidewalk stairway easy risers. View of Mt. Diablo.*

5   Waller/Broderick, into Buena Vista Park. *Garrett Eckbo was the architect of Buena Vista Park erosion-control measures, which include stairways. Work in progress. Hidden. View.*

CAYUGA

1   Rousseau/Alemany & Cayuga. *Across from the most visually stunning Dept. of Rec. & Park sculpture garden, park & playground in the City.*

CHINATOWN

A special combination of sounds, smells, and colors.

5   California/opposite No. 660, into St. Mary's Square. *A relatively low-rated stairway in a fascinating locale.*

5   Clay/Kearny & Grant, into Portsmouth Square.

DIAMOND HEIGHTS

A neighborhood of views, hills, and canyons.

4   Coralino/No. 289 Amber to No. 92 Cameo. *Woodsy. White-crowned sparrows love it.*

5   Diamond Heights Blvd/No. 687 28th St.

5   Moffitt at Diamond. *A very necessary stairway corner.*

5   Onique/No. 101 Berkeley—No. 289 Berkeley—No. 400 Gold Mine-Topaz. *45° view of San Francisco. Surroundings of eucalyptus, pine, canyons, hummingbirds. A four-tiered Chinese hopscotch walk.*

5   Opalo/No. 160 Gold Mine to Christopher Park. *Christopher Park is next to Diamond Heights shopping center.*

2   27th St/at No. 881 to No. 5150 Diamond Heights Blvd. Adjoining Douglass Playground. *Part of a long stairway outlined by trees. Nice access.*

DOLORES HEIGHTS

A lovely, hilly neighborhood in the Mission.

5   Cumberland/Noe & Sanchez. *Very impressive.*

4   Cumberland/Sanchez & Church. *View Hidden. Additional curving ramp and wall. Dense vegetation.*

5   Liberty/Noe & Rayburn. *Beautifully designed foliage plantings. Art Moderne houses alongside. View to east and west.*

3   19th St./over MUNI Metro into Dolores Park.

4   Sanchez/19th St. & Cumberland. *City-designed entrance stairway plus sidewalk stairs. At top, four large, 60-year-old cypresses alongside. View.*

5   Sanchez/Liberty & 21st St. *Network of stairs, one of the most beautiful series in the City. View.*

5   20th St. & Noe. Impressive. *Backdrop of high curving wall.*

5   20th St./Sanchez. *Two stairways descending gracefully. Views. Enter a cul-de-sac that connects with Noe stairway and ramp.*

DOWNTOWN

A neighborhood subject to significant changes.

2   Ellis/Market, down to BART/MUNI Metro station. *Rather steep.*

1   Embarcadero/Market, down into BART/MUNI Metro station. *Built in 1973. Concrete stairway and wall, brushed aluminum railings. Interesting new edifices of Financial District.*

2   Grant/Bush stairway & gate. *Entrance to Chinatown.*

2   Market/down into BART/MUNI Metro station. *Very steep.*

3   Montgomery/Market, down to BART/MUNI Metro station. *In the Financial District among historic and nonhistoric highrises. Bubbled tile wall.*

1 Powell/Geary, into Union Square. *Magicians, music, skits, street artists—lots of local color.*

4 Powell/Market, down to BART/MUNI Metro station. *Wide esplanade into Hallidie Plaza, near visitors information center.*

1 Stockton/Geary, into Union Square.

1 Stockton/Post, into Union Square.

2 Stockton/Sutter & Bush. *Over the Stockton Tunnel.*

2 Van Ness/Market, down to MUNI Metro station.

EDGEHILL

The steepness of the hill limits the number of homes on this street, which winds up to the summit.

3 Edgehill/Kensington—Granville—Allston—Dorchester.

5 Pacheco/Merced & Vasquez. *Echoes the Grand Stairway to the north.*

3 Vasquez/opposite No. 233 Kensington—Merced.

3 Verdun/Claremont—Lennox.

EMBARCADERO

Area undergoing revitalization since 1989 earthquake.

5 Commercial/Sansome & No. 1 Embarcadero Center. *Sculpture at entrance; concentric circle of tiles in pavement carry forward the visual pattern throughout the Embarcadero Center & Hyatt Regency Hotel. See sculpture and gardens throughout Center.*

4 Maritime Plaza/Washington/Clay/Battery/Front & Davis. *Six sets of stairways. Open space.*

EUREKA VALLEY

This neighborhood has a community organization active since 1881, a large gay population, fine Victorians, beautiful gardens, and the Castro—a movie palace built in 1922.

3 Caselli/Clayton & Market.

3 Collingwood/20th & 21st Sts. *Steep.*

4 Corwin/Douglas (400 block). *One of our favorite corners of the City.*

2   Dixie/Nos. 3795 & 3801 Market down to Grandview (across from No. 285).
1   Douglass & l9th.
4   Douglass/20th St. & Corwin. *Delightful discovery. Trees alongside. Exceptional.*
3   Douglass (No. 410 to No. 425). *Profuse plantings.*
4   Elizabeth/Hoffman & Grand View. *One of the grandest of the sidewalk stairways.*
3   No. 601 Grandview/24th St. & Cuesta Ct. *Hidden, Nicely planted area.*
2   Grandview/Market & Grandview Terrace.
3   Lamson Lane/Nos. 101 & 97 Caselli. *Cross alley. Continue up on variety of stairs—plaster, concrete, railroad tie & concrete, & partially covered bowl-shaped steps. Top of stairway/Nos. 4612 & 4608 19th St.*
3   Mono. Market to Eagle to Caselli.
2   Prosper/16th St. & Pond. *Behind Eureka branch library—an inviting place, a fine book collection.*
3   Romain/Douglass. *Upper to lower levels. Profuse plantings.*
3+ Seward/Douglass (No. 372). *Three sets of stairs. Enriches street by adding another level of viewing. Also very useful. Imaginative choice of plants. Beautiful corner of the city.*
3   21st St./Castro & Collingwood.
4   22nd St./Collingwood & Diamond. *Greenery all around*
3   22nd St./Collingwood & Castro. *Profuse plantings.*
3   Yukon/Eagle & Short. *Railroad-tie stairs into Kite Hill Park.*

EXCELSIOR

A stable neighborhood of diverse ethnic groups. Stairways reminiscent of the everyday kind in European towns.

2   Athens/Avalon & Valmar.
2   Campus Lane/Princeton & Burrows.
3   Dwight/Goettingen & Hamilton. *Very long. View.*
2   Excelsior/at No. 1021 into McLaren Park.
3   Excelsior/Munich & Prague.
2   Gladstone/Silver & Oxford.
3   Goettingen and Dwight.
2   Kenney Alley at No. 646 London to Mission. *Difficult to find.*
4   Munich/Ina & Excelsior. *Hidden. View. Osne of the newer (1977) stairways in the city.*

3 Munich/McLaren Park & Excelsior.

1 Naglee/Alemany & Cayuga. *At head of Cayuga Creek.*

4 Peru/Athens & Valmar. *Aggregate and railroad ties, designed by R. Schadt. Great views.*

3 Prague/Brazil & McLaren Park.

1 Restani/Cayuga & Alemany. *Practical. Hidden—only the residents know it.*

* Trumbull/Mission & Craut.

FOREST HILL

The City accepted responsibility for maintaining the non-regulation streets of this neighborhood.

4 Castenada at No. 140 to No. 334 Pacheco to No. 5 Sotelo. *Adjacent is a Maybeck house with delightful details, like the carved grapevines along the eaves.*

5 Montalvo/No. 376 Castenada—San Marcos—9th Ave—Mendosa. *Variety in terrain, architecture, and "custom-made" stairways.*

5 Pacheco/Magellan & No. 249 Castenada. *Grandest and most elegant of all San Francisco stairways.*

4 Alton/Pacheco at No. 400 to No. 60 Sotelo.

5 Alton/8th Ave. & No. 20 Ventura.

2 San Marcos/Dorantes. *Rounding a corner.*

5 Santa Rita at No. 60 to upper Pacheco at No. 349. *View of Marin.*

2 12th Ave./Magellan & Dorantes.

FOREST KNOLLS

A neighborhood heavily forested with eucalyptus.

4 Ashwood Stairway/Clarendon, No. 95 & No. 101 Warren. *Among the trees. View across to Mt. Davidson.*

4 Blairwood Lane/No. 109 Warren, No. 95 & No. 101 Crestmont. *View. With green railings it's almost camouflaged among pine and acacia. Floating stairs. Surreal view of TV tower.*

3 Glenhaven Lane/Oak Park & No. 191 Christopher.

5 Oakhurst Lane/Warren & Crestmont. *View of ocean. Difficult. Longest continuous stairway to highest elevation in San Francisco. Eucalyptus forest.*

FORT FUNSTON

Part of Golden Gate National Recreation Area. Off Hwy. 35, south of zoo.

4   "Horsetail" Stwy., left of parking lot. *Down along Pliocene-age cliffs, to ocean shore. Plan trip for low tide. Great view of hang-gliding activity.*

GLEN PARK

Cows roamed the meadowland in this neighborhood in the 1880s.

3   Amatista Lane/Bemis & Everson. *Hardy.*
2   Arlington at No. 439 to San Jose. *Hidden.*
3   Bemis/Addison & Miguel. Across from No. 41 Bemis.
2   Burnside/Bosworth.
2   Chilton/Bosworth & Lippard.
2   Cuvier/San Jose & Bosworth.
3   Diamond/Bosworth & Monterey into BART station. *View. Variety of textures in walks and stairs.*
2   Diamond/Moffitt.
2   Hamerton/Bosworth & Mangels.
1   Roanoke/San Jose & Arlington. *A walker's solution to freeway divisiveness.*
1   San Jose/Randall & Bosworth.
1   St. Mary's/San Jose & Arlington.

GOLDEN GATE HEIGHTS

Carl Larsen from Denmark deeded this acreage to the city in 1928.

3   Aerial Way/No. 475 Ortega & No. 801 Pacheco. *Long. Ice plants stabilize soil. Part of a network of stairways, all rated 4 or 5.*
2   Aloha and Lomita.
5   Cascade Walk/Ortega, Pacheco & Funston. *Secluded. Special.*
3   Crestwell/off Ortega.
3   Encinal Walk/14th & 15th Avenues.
4   15th Ave./Kirkham & Lomita. *View.*
4   15th Ave./Kirkham & Lawton. *Pine trees alongside. Walk up slowly.*
4   14th Ave./Pacheco. *Very long trek up.*
4   Lomita/Kirkham & Lawton. *View of houses on stilts.*

4 Mandalay Lane/No. 2001 14th & 15th Aves. & Pacheco. *Ocean view.*
5 Moraga/west from 12th Ave., east from 17th Ave.
4 Mount Lane/No. 1795 14th Ave. and No. 1798 15th Ave.
4 Noriega/15th Ave. & Sheldon Terrace. *Huge rock outcropping.*
4 Oriole Way/Pacheco & Cragmont. *Lots of foliage and long landings. View of houses on stilts.*
4 Ortega Way/14th Ave. & No. 1894 15th Ave. *Very long and very practical. Ocean view Ice plants on sides.*
4 Pacheco/15th Ave. *View.*
2 Pacheco & 14th Ave. *Rounding a corner.*
4 No. 500 Quintara/14th & 15th Aves. *Great sunset viewing area. Double stairway a third of the way. Built 1928. View.*
3 Quintara at corner of 16th Ave. *Nice curving wide-rounded corner.*
5 Selma Way/No. 477 Noriega & No. 564 Ortega. *View. High, high, high.*
3 16th Ave./Kirkham & Lawton. *Stairway built before the surrounding houses.*
3 16th Ave/Pacheco & Quintara. *Series of small stairways. Graceful.*
5 12th Ave/Cragmont, into Golden Gate Heights Park. *Cobblestone stairs.*

GOLDEN GATE PARK

Stairs still being built here.

3 Anglers Lodge/off Kennedy Dr., opposite Buffalo Paddock. *Stone stairway.*
3 Arboretum near Sunset Garden.
3 Children's Playground to Kezar Dr.
3 Conservatory (east of). Dahlia gardens. *Concrete stairs.*
3 Fulton & 10th Ave. *Wide railroad-tie/blacktop stairs. Into play and rest area. Designed by Walter Kocian.*
3 Fulton & 8th Ave. *Side of DeYoung Museum.*
3 Fulton & Arguello. *Curving railroad-tie stairs and sides.*
3 Horseshoe Court. *Built in the 1930s.*
3 Huntington Falls/top of Strawberry Hill to Stow Lake. *Railroad-tie & chicken-wire boxes filled with boulders and stones. A stairway for giants and a giant waterfall.*
2 Japanese Tea Garden to north side of Stow Lake.
2 South Dr. (Martin Luther King Dr.) near Murphy Windmill to Great Highway. *Continues to footpath.*

2   South Dr. (Martin Luther King Dr.) to Big Rec. area.

2   South Dr. (Martin Luther King Dr.) to Stow Lake.

3   South Dr. (Main Luther King Dr.)/intersection of Kennedy Dr. Wooden. *Leads to footpath.*

3   Stow Lake/south side, to south side of Strawberry Hill. *Wooden stairs.*

5   Strawberry Hill from top to Stow Lake shore. *Fine view. Built of railroad ties, will connect with two new stairways, one on each side of Huntington Falls.*

INGLESIDE TERRACE

3   San Leandro/Moncado (No. 344) & Ocean. *44 stairs.*

3   Wyton/Denslowe & 19th Ave. (footpath/stairway).

LANDS END

Great area for ocean breezes and beaches.

4   Eagle's Point/Coastal Trail & the ocean.

3   Lands End Stwy./lower footpath & Fort Miley parking.

4   Mile Rock/Coastal Trail & the ocean. *One of the new stairways.*

5   Milestone Stwy./Merrie Way & Sutro Baths. *Railroad tie.*

4   Naval Memorial Stwy./48th Ave. & El Camino Del Mar.

5   Sutro Heights Park: 48th Ave/Point Lobos Ave. & Anza. *21-acre estate of Adolph Sutro, purchased in 1881. Stone stairway to ramparts offers excellent ocean views.*

MARINA

Development of this neighborhood was given impetus from the 1915 International Exposition.

3   Fort Mason/Bateria San Jose & picnic areas.

3   Fort Mason/Great Meadow to piers, opposite Bldg. E.

3   Fort Mason/picnic area & Pier 3.

4   Fort Mason/upper fort to Aquatic Park. *View.*

4   Jefferson/Beach, Hyde & Larkin.

MISSION

One of the largest districts in San Francisco. Divided into more than a dozen sub-neighborhoods.

3   17th St./Potrero & Bryant, into Franklin Square.
3   16th St./Bryant, into Franklin Square.
3   24th St./Mission, down in BART station.

MOUNT DAVIDSON

A neighborhood circling the highest elevation in San Francisco. The Cross and the surrounding plateau are now privately owned.

3   Bengal/Miraloma & Lansdale. *Wooden risers, concrete & cobblestone steps.*
3   Burlwood/Los Palmos. *Rounding a corner.*
4   Dalewood Way, from Mt. Davidson. *Stone & moss stairways along nature trails of pine and eucalyptus.*
4   Detroit/Joost, Monterey & Hearst. *Very handy. A street stairway crossing a main thoroughfare. Compare with Harry St.*
2   Globe Alley/No. 96 Cresta Vista to Hazelwood near Los Palmos. *Combination easement and stairway.*
2   Lulu Alley/Los Palmos & No. 450—No. 500 Melrose. *Combination easement and stairway.*
4   Melrose/Teresita to Mangels to Sunnyside Playground. Starts down from No. 195 Melrose. *Much variety in the stair series. Melrose is a double street! The 800 block of Teresita is across from No. 195 Melrose.*
3   Miraloma/Portola. *Follows pedestrian skyway to West Portal neighborhood.*
3   Myra/No. 95 Coventry & Dalewood. *Hidden. Curved & grooved lane.*
4   Rex/Juanita & Mane. *Fog, moss, stone, and fresh air.*
3   Yerba Buena/Ravenwood.

NOB HILL

A famous neighborhood well-known to tourists.

4   Joice/Pine, Sacramento, Powell & Stockton. *Graceful curve at Pine.*
2   Mason/southeast corner of California.
2   Priest, opposite No. 1350 Washington, to Clay.

2   Reid/Washington & Clay. *Connects to Priest Stwy.*

3   Sacramento/Taylor & Mason into Huntington Park.

3   Taylor/California & Sacramento into Huntington Park.

3   Taylor/Pine & California. *Sidewalk stairway on both sides of the street, 235 steps.*

NOE VALLEY

An authentic neighborhood.

4   Castro/28th & Duncan. *Panoramic views. Franciscan rock formation. Wildlife haven. Strenuous walking.*

3   Castro/Day & No. 590 30th Sts. *We have non-streets and double streets and stairways intersecting. Adjacent Franciscan rock cliffs. Entrance to Glen Park neighborhood.*

5   Cumberland/Noe. *Cobblestone wall. Zigzag contour of stairs. View.*

3   No. 493 Day up to No. 2350 Castro. *Go up.*

3   Diamond/Valley. *Wildlife haven. Great moon-viewing lookout. Panoramic view.*

2   Duncan/Noe toward Sanchez. *Duncan is so steep that it is free of traffic from here to Diamond.*

5   Harry at No. 190 Beacon to Laidley. *Unusual stairway that connects to Noe Valley, Glen Park, maybe Diamond Heights, too. Secluded. Built in 1932 by Eaton & Smith, Contractors.*

2   Noe/Army & 27th St. *Sidewalk stairway.*

4   Liberty/Sanchez & Church. *Stairways here. Very inviting area, lots of foliage.*

2   Sanchez/Cumberland.

4   22nd St./Church & Vicksburg. *Sidewalk stairway. If you feel you're sliding backward, it's because the steps slope backward. One of the steepest climbs in the city.*

3   27th St./Castro & Newburg. *Views. Stairway at end of cul-de-sac is blocked off.*

2   Valley/Castro to Noe. *Steep driveways show height of original street.*

NORTH BEACH

A neighborhood in transition from predominantly Italian settlers to Chinese.

2 Brenham Pl./Washington & Kearny.

4 Jack Early Park. *An oasis for contemplation.*

2 Romolo/Vallejo & Fresno, west of Kearny.

3 Tuscany/Lombard. *Like the Winchester Mystery House stairs, these go nowhere.*

PACIFIC HEIGHTS

A neighborhood that has maintained standards in architecture and appearance. Enviable views and private schools.

5 Baker/Vallejo & Broadway. *Plantings of Monterey pine, marguerites, hebe. Walk on the west side and experience stair walking vs uphill walking!*

4 Broderick/Broadway & Vallejo. *One of the few stairways whose designer is known: Schubert & Friedman, 1979. View.*

3 Across from No. 1171 Clay/Washington, Sproul & Taylor.

3 Fillmore/Green & Vallejo. *Sidewalk stairway, presented by the Fillmore Street Improvement Association in 1915.*

3 Gough/Clay, into Lafayette Park. *Near tennis courts.*

3 Gough/Washington, into Lafayette Park.

4 Green/Scott & Pierce. *Stairway imbedded in center of wide sidewalk.*

3 Laguna/Washington, into Lafayette Park. *Sunbathers in summer.*

5 Lyon/Green & Vallejo & Broadway. *Designed by Louis Upton, 1916. View. Complete arrangement of stairs, planting areas, landings.*

4 Normandie Ter./Vallejo. *Built in 1938, not accepted by the city until 1976.*

3 Octavia/Washington & Jackson. *Surrounded by mansions. Stairways within cul-de-sac. Obviously planned, but for what?*

5 Pierce/Clay & Washington, into Alta Plaza. *Beautifully proportioned, extremely wide, tiered. Amid low shrubbery and lawn. Designed by John McLaren.*

3 Pierce/Jackson & Washington, into Alta Plaza. *Sunny. View to North Bay.*

3 Sacramento/Laguna & Gough, into Lafayette Park. *Stairway originally went to house of one Holladay, a squatter! Dog-run area nearby.*

5 Scott/Clay & Washington, into Alta Plaza. *Elegant stairway surrounded by elaborate Victorians.*

5 Steiner/Clay & Washington, into Alta Plaza. *Beginning a series of wide stairs.*

5   Steiner/Washington & Jackson, into Alta Plaza. *Imposing entrance.*
    Benches and paths to four corners of the park.
3   Vallejo/Scott & Pierce. *Sidewalk stairway.*
3   Webster/Broadway & Vallejo. *Sidewalk stairway across from Flood*
    Mansion, which is now a private school.

PARNASSUS HEIGHTS

Home of UC Medical School, with Sutro Forest, once Ishi's preserve, as
the background.

3   Farnsworth/Edgewood & Willard. *Beautiful and meandering.*
3   Kirkham/4th Ave. up to 1550 5th Ave. Behind UC Medical School.
    Wood stairway. Hidden in the woods.

PORTOLA

A neighborhood showing strains.

3   Beeman Lane/Wabash & San Bruno.
3   Campbell/San Bruno & Bayshore.
3   San Bruno & Arletta.
3   Sunglow Lane/Gladstone & Silver.

POTRERO HILL

Beautiful weather and views.

3   Army/Evans & Mississippi.
3   Carolina/19th & 20th Sts. *Views of Bay Bridge and freeway network.*
    Embankment plantings by Victoria Mews Assoc. Beautiful. Secluded.
2   Mariposa/Utah & Potrero. *Sidewalk stairway.*
*   Missouri/opposite No. 571 near Sierra, to Texas. *Two stairways going*
    nowhere.
3   22nd St./Arkansas & Wisconsin. *Rural. View.*
2   22nd St./Kansas & Rhode Island. *Sidewalk stairway. Very steep.*
4   Vermont/20th to 22nd St. Curly street. *Several stairways radiating*
    from successive cul-de-sacs. Stairway to McKinley Square. Great view.
4   San Bruno/20th St.
4   McKinley Park. *Four stairways into park; two into park from San Bruno.*

4   San Bruno/ 18th St.

PRESIDIO

Founded in 1776 by the Spanish under the leaders, Moraga and Anza.

3   Barnard/Hicks, up to Presidio Blvd. *Good for exploring.*
2   Presidio Blvd./MacArthur Ave. & Letterman Blvd. *Series of small stair-ways.*
3   Lincoln Blvd./Pershing Dr. & Cobb Ave. to Baker Beach. *Logs and chain. Excellent view of Golden Gate.*

RICHMOND

Known as the "sand waste" area in early days of San Francisco.

5   California/32nd Ave. & golf course, to Lincoln Park. *Surrounded by cypresses. 29'-wide stairway with landings, benches. Footpath around to the Legion of Honor.*
5   El Camino Del Mar/Palace of the Legion of Honor. *Come here for the setting; it's unsurpassed. Many paths to explore in this national urban park.*
1   48th Ave./Balboa & Sutro Heights. *Magnificent view of Pacific Ocean; take stairs on right-hand side. In front of No. 680 48th, well-worn foot-path up to Sutro Heights.*
4   Lake/El Camino Del Mar to 30th Ave. *Stairways between three levels of Lake. Very pretty.*
4   Seacliff/from No. 330 toward China Beach. *In the elegant Seacliff neighborhood.*
4   27th Ave./Seacliff & El Camino Del Mar. *Beautiful area. Four brick stairways.*

RUSSIAN HILL

Grave of Russians buried on the hill account for the neighborhood name.

5   Chestnut/Polk & Larkin. *In center of Chestnut cul-de-sac. Very wide. Foliage. Double staircase up to Larkin.*
3   Culebra Ter./No. 1256 Lombard & Chestnut. *Charming. Terraced.*

5   Filbert/Hyde & Leavenworth. *Sidewalk stairway. Coit Tower straight ahead. 124 steps. Strenuous walk up a 31.5° grade.*

3   Florence/Broadway & Vallejo. *Charming. Pueblo Revival houses near the 1939 stairway.*

5   Upper Francisco/Upper Leavenworth & Hyde. *Ivy cascading down walls, urns, view to the north, pines.*

4   Green/Jones & Taylor. Next to No. 940 Green.

5   Greenwich/Hyde & Larkin. *Set into tennis courts.*

5   Greenwich/Hyde & Leavenworth. *View.*

5   Greenwich (south side)/Leavenworth & Jones. *Michelangelo Park. Neighborhood activist, Nan McGuire, spearheaded extraordinary transformation of ugly space into esthetic multi-use park with stairways, plants, tables, benches, community garden, play equipment.*

4   Havens/Leavenworth & Hyde. *In cul-de-sac, with entrance only on west side of Leavenworth. Charming.*

2   Himmelman Pl./Mason & Taylor to Broadway. *Utilitarian, with mini-park alongside.*

1   Houston/Jones & Columbus. Next to No. 2430 Jones.

3   Hyde and Francisco. *Deeply grooved corner stair—necessary.*

5   Jones/Filbert & Union & Green. *Nicely proportioned. Raised sidewalk stairway. Hard work. Stairs have a visual pattern of horizontal louvered shades.*

4   Larkin/Bay & Francisco. *Long series of stairs. Pass by reservoir paths.*

3   Larkin/Chestnut & Francisco to Bay. Begins at No. 2745 Larkin. *View of reservoir and slope of vegetation.*

4   Leavenworth/Chestnut & Francisco. *Walk on west side to long rampart; try both upper and lower approach.*

5   Lombard/Hyde & Leavenworth. *Curly here, straight there.*

2/5 Macondray Lane/Leavenworth & Jones, Union & Green. *The eastern section of Macondray is Shangri-la; the western is not.*

3   Montclair Ter./Lombard & Chestnut. *Hidden.*

5   Vallejo/Jones & Taylor. *Retaining wall dates to 1914. View. Entrance to special section of Vallejo that has historic value: Willis Polk designed houses on Russian Hill Place and stairway entrance on Jones.*

5   Vallejo/Mason & Taylor. *Winding.*

2   Valparaiso/Filbert & Greenwich on Taylor.

SOUTH OF MARKET

Once an early residential neighborhood—subsequently industrial, presently mixed.

3 Beale/Main & Fremont to Harrison. *Ed. Beale was the first to bring gold samples to the east coast, in 1848. On old Rincon Hill, anchor of the Bay Bridge.*

* Lansing/First Street & Essex. *Freeway fumes with every breath. Once (in Gold Rush times) this was an elegant neighborhood.*

4 Yerba Buena Gardens/Mission & Howard, 3rd & 4th Sts. *The area, after 30 years of being a civic eyesore, has evolved into the pride of San Francisco. 5 ½-acre park, galleries, butterfly gardens, outdoor sculptures, 20'-high waterfall.*

ST. FRANCIS WOOD

Architect-designed gates and fountains at boulevard entrance.

3 Junipero Serral/9th Ave.

2 Miraloma/Yerba Buena.

2 Miraloma/Upper Yerba Buena.

3 Portola/Claremont.

3 Portola/Santa Clara. Across from No. 1420 Portola. West of Vicente. Near Terrace.

1 Stonestown Stwy./l9th Ave. & Stonestown Center. *Across from Mercy High School.*

5 Terrace Walk /San Anselmo & Yerba Buena. *Newly rebuilt of solid redwood, amid trees and park land.*

3 San Anselmo/St. Francis & San Andreas.

SUNNYSIDE

Neighborhood worth exploring.

5 Next to No. 233 Joost down to Monterey Blvd., via historic Sunnyside Conservatory. *Unusual landscaping designed by Ted Kipping, neighbor and arborist.*

TELEGRAPH HILL

Early photos show stairways literally hanging over the cliffs of this historic neighborhood. Three new stairways leading to Coit Tower in progress.

2   Bartol Alley at No. 379 Broadway, to Montgomery & Prescott. *Franciscan Formation under an adjacent house.*

4   Calhoun/upper to lower Union & Montgomery. *View is an unexpected eye-opener.*

3   Child/Lombard & Telegraph Pl. *Almost unseen. Form and function in accord.*

5   Filbert/Grant & Kearny. Next to Garfield School. *Steps of perfect proportion.*

3   Filbert/Kearny.

5   Filbert/Telegraph Hill Blvd., Montgomery & Sansome. *Part of Historic District. Wonderful, extensive plantings.*

4   Francisco/Kearny & Grant. *An attractive access to Coit Tower.*

2   Genoa Place/Union, Kearny & Varennes.

4   Greenwich/Grant & Kearny. *An attractive way up to the summit of the hill and Coit Tower.*

5   Greenwich/Telegraph Blvd. & Montgomery & Sansome. *Unusual trees in the canyon.*

4   Grant/Francisco & Pfeiffer St. *Jack Early Park. An oasis for neighborhood residents and others. Perfect for moon viewing.*

3   Julius Street/Lombard & Whiting. *Not easily seen.*

3   Kearny/Francisco. *Wooden stairs that begin in a garden setting and end in a gardened cul-de-sac, with an unusual elevated walkway in between.*

5   Kearny/Lombard & Telegraph Hill Blvd. *View.*

4   Kearny/Vallejo & Broadway. *Total pedestrian block. Strenuous. Adjacent post-1906 houses are unfortunately disappearing.*

5   Lombard/Kearny & Telegraph Hill Blvd. *View.*

4   Montgomery/Green & Union.

3   Montgomery/Union & Greenwich.

3   Pardee Alley near Grant to Greenwich.

2   San Antonio Pl./Vallejo to Kearny & Grant.

4   Union/Calhoun & east cliff of Telegraph Hill. *Close-up of geologic formation of the hill. View.*

3   Vallejo/Montgomery & Kearny. *Angled and & tiered. Plantings throughout.*

TWIN PEAKS

A focal point for the entire city as outlined in the 1905 Burnham Beautification report, Ideas discarded in the mad rush to rebuild after the 1906 earthquake and fire.

2   Burnett/opposite No. 535, upper to lower.
4   Clayton/Corbett. *View. Lovely transitional stairway. Fine specimen of a corner-stairway design.*
3   Clayton/Market. *Graceful corner stairway.*
3   Copper/Greystone & Corbett, next to No. 301 Greystone & No. 592 Corbett. *Extraordinary view. Stairway in the process of disappearing.*
2   Crestline at No. 70, to Parkridge. *View.*
2   Cuesta Court to Corbett.
4   Cuesta Court/Portola & Corbett. *Exceptional view. Cotoneaster and Monterey pines.*
2   Fredela Ln./Clairview Ct. & Fairview Ct.
2   Fredela Ln./Lower Marview & Clairview Ct.
2   Gardenside/Burnett. *View.*
2   Gardenside/Parkridge. *Glorious views.*
5   Pemberton Pl./Crown & Clayton. *Compelling view. 1942-vintage stairway. 1995 redesign. Stamped-concrete stairs, terra-cotta color; handrails, lights. Designed by Brian Gatter. Lower stairway & wall under renovation.*
3   Stanyan, near No. 1289, up to Belgrave (formerly up to Clarendon).
3   Twin Peaks Blvd., next to No. 192 (opposite Crown Terrace), up to Tank Hill. *Panoramic view.*

UPPER MARKET

The neighborhood is enjoying a renaissance. Gardens and houses are being renovated by community groups.

4   Ashbury, next to No. 64. *(1911–1912 development).*
2   Church/Market, down into MUNI Metro station. *Terrazzo stairway, ceramic tile walls.*
2   Clifford Terrace/Roosevelt. *Rounding the corner.*
4   Corbett at No. 336. *Behind it is a long alley and stairway.*
1   Corbett/17th St. *The two steps serve the purpose of rounding the corner.*
3   Corbin Place/17th St. & Corbett.
3   Danvers/18th St. & Market. *A 1946 stairway.*

3   Douglass/States & 17th St. *Charming, tree-lined cul-de-sac with an assortment of Victorians.*

2   Glendale/Corbett.

3   Grandview, next to No. 600, to Market. *View. Accompaniment to modified skywalk. Well-planted area.*

4   Henry/No. 473 Roosevelt & Castro. *Cul-de-sac. Hidden. A charmer.*

3   Iron Alley/No. 495 Corbett to No. 1499 Clayton, and extension to Market & Graystone. *Unusual view from below. Wooden stairs. If you don't suffer from agoraphobia, walk down from Corbett and experience city elevations.*

3   Levant/States & Roosevelt. *High retaining wall covered with vines. Butterflies and chickadees abound in the foliage. Curved street complements stairs.*

3   Lower Terrace/Saturn. *Four short stairways that connect with Saturn/Ord Stwy.*

2   Market/Grand *View. Hidden. Watch out for tree trunks.*

4   Market/Short.

4   Mono/Eagle & Market. *Part of a long twitton.*

3   Monument Way/Mt. Olympus. *View. You're at the geographical center of San Francisco.*

4   Monument Way/Upper Terrace. *View. Neighborly.*

1   Ord Ct. at No. 2 to Douglass cul-de-sac. *Surprise.*

3   Ord St./Storrie & Market down to Ord & 18th St. *Happy wall mural on No. 176 Ord at end of stairway.*

2   Roosevelt/17th St. *Rounding a corner.*

3   Roosevelt Way/Lower Ter. *Cotoneaster shrubs alongside.*

4   Saturn/Ord & 17th St. *Redesigned by Department of Public Works. Benches & planted areas augment curving stairway.*

2   Saturn/Temple & 100 block of Saturn. *Three series of four to five steps down to street. Good use of stair idea.*

3   17th St./Clayton & Roosevelt to Upper Ter. *Alongside large apartment buildings. Goes to a concentric circle where the view is fabulous.*

2   17th St./Corbett. *Rounding the corner.*

2   17th. St./Mars. *Rounding a corner.*

2   17th St./Roosevelt. *Rounding a corner.*

3   Stanton/Grand View & Market. *Hidden. Will soon be an archaeological find.*

4   Temple/Corbett & 17th St. Next to No. 4399 17th. *Tiered plantings on both sides of stairs.*

5   Vulcan/Levant & Ord. *Not to be missed. Caring neighbors. Cobblestone terracing.*

WESTERN ADDITION

This neighborhood survived the 1906 earthquake and grew and grew until it reached its peak during World War II.

* Arbol Lane/Turk & Anza Vista. *A street stairway.*
* Fulton/Steiner, into Alamo Square.
* Grove/Scott & Steiner, into Alamo Square.
* Hayes/Scott & Pierce. *Divided street, several stairways.*
* Pierce/Fulton, into Alamo Square.
* Sonora Lane/O'Farrell & Terra Vista.
* Steiner/Grove & Hayes, into Alamo Square.

Index

Author Note

Adah Bakalinsky grew up in St. Paul, Minnesota, surrounded by flat land. Then the family moved to Pleasant Avenue, near Ramsey Hill. She remembers trying to walk up the icy hill in winter, slithering down, trying again, and finally reaching the top. Fifty years later, while on a visit and walking in the old neighborhood, she discovered a stairway had been built to ascend the hill!

Looking for a synthesis for her social work, music, and film background, she discovered, surprisingly, that it was walking. She walks, and as she walks she talks to whomever will talk with her. She carries a tape recorder to capture stories; she finds that walks shape themselves into a variety of musical forms and dances, and she redesigns a walk until it has just the rhythm it must have. She walks to see, and returns to photograph the objects that give flavor to the walk. She feels lucky to live in San Francisco, where walking seems the most natural way to traverse the City.

NOTES